D0919028

Joe Petrosino

Joe Petrosino

by Arrigo Petacco

Translated by Charles Lam Markmann

MACMILLAN PUBLISHING CO., INC.

NEW YORK

Library of Congress Cataloging in
Publication Data

Petacco, Arrigo.
  Joe Petrosino.

    1. Petrosino, Joseph, 1860–1909.
HV7911.P45P4813   364.1'523'0924 [B]
73-17179
ISBN 0-02-595160-2

English translation copyright © 1974 by
Macmillan Publishing Co., Inc.

All rights reserved. No part of this book may be
reproduced or transmitted in any form or by any
means, electronic or mechanical, including
photocopying, recording or by any information
storage and retrieval system, without permission in
writing from the Publisher.

Macmillan Publishing Co., Inc.
866 Third Avenue, New York, N.Y. 10022
Collier-Macmillan Canada Ltd.

FIRST AMERICAN EDITION 1974

Joe Petrosino was published in the Italian language
in 1972 by Mondadori Publishing Company, Inc.,
Milan. © Arnoldo Mondadori Editore 1972

Printed in the United States of America

TO *Monica* AND *Carlotta*

Contents

Joe Petrosino

1. The Man in the Barrel

THE WIDOW CARMELINA NISCEMI ZILLO leaned cautiously out the window of the one-room apartment that she shared with her four children. It was six o'clock in the morning, April 14, 1903; East Eleventh Street, in the Italian section of New York, lay empty below her. The barest echoes of early traffic came from nearby Third Avenue. With considerable circumspection, Carmelina leaned out farther to take a careful look at the street and the houses on the other side. Then, when she was quite sure that no one was watching her, she snatched up a bucket of garbage and hurled its contents out the window.

She did the same thing every morning, even though she knew that the police acted very harshly against anyone who dirtied the streets. Besides, Carmelina was not the only one who was guilty of this offense every day. Five storys down, in the vacant lot next to the house, there was a mountain of refuse that had obviously been thrown from many other windows too.

Carmelina put away the bucket and looked out the window again with an air of unconcern. "If the street-cleaners don't come today either, we'll wind up with an epidemic," she said half-aloud, eying the heap of filth with disgust. At this moment her attention was arrested by something odd just beside the pile. She looked harder, and in the grey light of early morning she made out a large barrel standing upright at the inner edge of the sidewalk.

To a mother who is a widow, a foreigner, and poor, a barrel can be a thing of a thousand uses if it is in good condition. And, since Carmelina was indeed just such a mother, she ran downstairs quickly, hoping no potential rival would get there ahead of her. The house door opened onto Third Avenue, already becoming crowded with working men and domestics on their way to jobs in upper areas of Manhattan. Carmelina pulled her black shawl closer round her head and turned the corner into Eleventh Street to get to the vacant lot that was the garbage dump for the many Italian immigrant families that lived in the old tenement.

Tall and broad, with new staves and with hoops that had barely begun to rust, the barrel was still where she had seen it. Carmelina tried several times to move it, without success. Not only was the barrel not empty; it was unbelievably heavy. Her curiosity aroused, the woman began tugging at the lid of the barrel and finally she managed to lift it. Then she looked inside, screamed once, and fainted.

A few minutes later, drawn by the scream, a few passers-by and a policeman from the Second District came on the scene. The policeman, an Irish-American named John O'Brien, went and looked inside the barrel, at which Carmelina, still speechless, was pointing frantically. The sight was upsetting for O'Brien too; sticking out of the sawdust in the barrel was a man's head with his genitals in his mouth.

The "case of the man in the barrel," as the crime came to be known in the New York newspaper headlines, came within the jurisdiction of the Second District, under the command of Inspector

David Schmittberger. It was clear from the outset that it was going to be a very difficult case.

The man had been stabbed to death before the mutilation.* But on the body, which had been taken in its primitive coffin to the Second District's headquarters in Union Market, the police found no papers that would enable them to establish the victim's identity or even his nationality. After a preliminary examination, however, the inspector came to the conclusion that the victim must have been of Mediterranean origin, probably a Greek or an Armenian. He stated also that it was his conviction that he was dealing with a ritual murder, some kind of human sacrifice carried out by one of the innumerable secret sects that Easterners had brought to the New World. This conviction was bolstered when a search of the victim's pockets produced a small gilt crucifix engraved "I.N.R.I." Schmittberger, a Jew, did not recognize the initials and mistakenly took them for the symbol of the sect to which the victim must have belonged.

Later, when the evening papers were already reporting the most fantastic theories as to the character of the crime, a policeman going through the dead man's clothes for the nth time came across a rolled-up bit of paper on which a sentence was written in Italian. "Come at once; it's important," the message read. But not a man in the Second District understood Italian; and it was only later, with the help of an Italian shopkeeper on Mulberry Street, that it was possible to translate the terse message.

At this point Schmittberger abandoned the defense of his theory. "Maybe I guessed wrong," he told a colleague named McCafferty. "This must be some Italian business. The best thing would be to send for The Dago."

The Dago was the nickname generally applied in police circles to Detective Joseph (born Giuseppe) Petrosino, the only policeman of Italian origin who had risen as high as the Homicide Bureau, the office headed by the five most able investigators in New York.

Within an hour, a thickset man wearing a dark suit and a derby

---

*Because of the mutilation, the crime also came to be known later, and inaccurately, as "the case of the man who was cut to pieces."—Author.

hat and carrying a cane walked into the Second District offices. His hard square face was lightly marked by smallpox.

"My name is Petrosino," he said somewhat pompously to the policeman on desk duty, whereupon he was shown into the improvised morgue in which the murdered man's body was being kept. Petrosino nodded to Schmittberger and got right down to business without wasting time on amenities.

Having examined the corpse with a meticulousness that seemed exaggerated to Schmittberger, inasmuch as he himself had already examined it several times, Petrosino turned his attention to the man's clothes, pulling the pockets inside out and shaking dust from them into an envelope. Then he examined the barrel. He wrote down in his notebook the letters stamped on the lid—W.T.—poked at the cracks between the staves with a penknife, found some white dust that he tested with the tip of his tongue, and, finally, thrust his cane into the mass of sawdust in which the gruesome contents had been packed. The sawdust was very dirty, and full of pieces of paper and a large number of cigarette and cigar butts. The detective inspected everything very carefully. "This is a *toscano*,"* he muttered to himself when he picked up a cigar fragment. Then he asked a policeman to fill a bag for him with a few handfuls of the sawdust; he wanted to examine it more thoroughly later.

When he had finished his work, Petrosino turned to Inspector Schmittberger: "I'd like to look at the other things you found on the body," he said.

Schmittberger ushered the detective into his office and took the note and the crucifix from a locked drawer. "This is a clue," Petrosino said, putting the piece of paper into his pocket. "But this is of no use to me," he added, handing back the crucifix.

"But the lettering . . . look at the lettering!" Schmittberger cried in amazement.

Petrosino, who never laughed, allowed himself a hint of a smile. "The letters stand for *Iesus Nazarenus Rex Iudaeorum*,"** he ex-

*A specific type of cheap and very strong Italian cigar.—Translator.
**Jesus of Nazareth, King of the Jews—the mocking legend supposedly placed on the cross by the Romans at the crucifixion.—Translator.

plained, "and they mean that Jesus is your king, even if you Jews don't think so."

Schmittberger took it without resentment. He even managed to laugh.

Petrosino rose to leave. "I'll send you somebody from the Bureau to take a picture of the body. I hope you can fix it up so the photograph will be decent."

"I'll get somebody from an undertaker's," Schmittberger said. "They're artists at these things."

"Good," the detective said. "And it would be a good thing too to track down a firm that uses 'W.T.' as its trademark. It would have to be a candy or pastry maker, because the inside of the barrel has sugar on it."

Impressed by the detective's requests, Schmittberger promised to do his best. Then he asked whether Petrosino intended to make a statement to the reporters who had been hanging about outside the Second District all day.

Petrosino agreed readily; he was always very responsive to the needs of the press. Besides, it had really been the newspapers that had made him the best-known policeman in New York. So on the evening of April 14, Joseph Petrosino gave out a statement on the case.

"The man in the barrel," he said, "was certainly an Italian and probably a Sicilian. I think he was murdered to settle a quarrel in some gang or other. In Sicily, from what I know, the business of stuffing the genitals into the mouth is used on people who talk too much."

One reporter asked him whether the crime could be attributed to the "Black Hand," the criminal organization that was terrorizing the Italian section. Petrosino replied, nettled: "I've told you many times before that the 'Black Hand' doesn't exist as a functioning organization. It's the newspapers that have built up the myth of an octopus that's supposed to have the whole city of New York in its tentacles. What does actually exist is gangs, mostly very small, and not connected with one another, that have appropriated this name that the anarchists invented to frighten their victims."

When he had finished with the reporters, Joseph Petrosino went back to police headquarters, then at 300 Mulberry Street in the heart of the Italian quarter. There he got a phone call from Inspector Schmittberger, who made no attempt to conceal his excitement as he announced that he had found the firm that marked its barrels "W.T."

"It's a confectionery called Wallace & Towney, located at 365 Washington Street," Schmittberger said. "They make various kinds of pastries, mainly for pushcart peddlers, but they also supply some restaurants, using those very barrels. Two of those places," the inspector concluded, "are saloons in my district. One of them is a German *Bierstube* on Prince Street and the other is the Star of Italy Bar, run by a man named Pietro Inzerillo and located at 260 Elizabeth Street."

Petrosino, who had been taking notes rapidly, thanked Schmittberger and hung up. Now the matter was beginning to be a little clearer.

A little before midnight the detective got out of a carriage outside the Star of Italy—he had immediately ruled out the German saloon. His appearance produced the usual stir that always followed his entrance into any of the many smoky bars that served as meeting-places for Italian underworld figures. The Star of Italy was one of them.

Petrosino recognized, sitting at the tables where they were playing cards, bottles of wine at hand, a great number of gangsters who in his view ought to have been thrown out of the country or into prison, but who enjoyed complete freedom of movement because of what he considered the excessive concern of American laws for the rights of the individual.

As usual the policeman took a corner table so that his back was against the wall, and then ordered a drink. He sat there without moving for some ten minutes. He wanted to create the impression that this was just one of his customary visits to keep an eye on things.

He had noted on entering that the floor of the restaurant was covered with a layer of sawdust, which gave the customers full freedom to spit. It was precisely this sawdust that interested him most. Pretending to tie a loose shoelace, he bent down, scooped up a few pinches of the sawdust and emptied them into his trouser cuff.

When he was out in the street again he walked round the building. At the back, where the bar had its service door, several big barrels were stacked. All of them bore the trademark of Wallace & Towney.

The next day, an expert on the staff of the modest scientific laboratory that had recently been set up at New York City's Police Headquarters assured Petrosino that the sawdust he had gathered at the Star of Italy was identical with that in the barrel.

With this the solution of the case seemed quite near. Obviously the man had been killed in that cutthroats' headquarters, the Star of Italy, and then left in plain sight on Eleventh Street so that— following Sicilian custom—those for whom it was meant would get the lesson of what "spies" could expect. On this point Petrosino had no doubt whatever. He was much too familiar with the ways of the East Side Italian underworld. He knew, too, that killers resorted to such melodramatic arrangements only when they meant to put out a "warning." They preferred to dispose of ordinary murder victims by sinking them in the East River with blocks of concrete attached to their feet as insurance. Now Petrosino had to find a name for "the man in the barrel." Only by identifying him would he be able to find out who had killed him.

Preliminary investigation kept Petrosino occupied for several days. It appears from the archives that hundreds of Italians were brought in to look at the body in the hope that some of them might recognize it. But it was a waste of effort. One Sicilian, Michele Bongiorno by name, identified the victim as a certain Antonino Quattrocchi, the son-in-law of a notorious smuggler of illegal aliens. But, just as the news of his murder was about to be officially released, Quattrocchi turned up of his own volition, hale and hearty, at Police Headquarters.

This incident was at once exploited to the full by the many little Italian rags in New York that never missed an opportunity to discredit the work of police investigators (as they had done earlier in the matter of the crucifix bearing the "mysterious initials"). Even Petrosino became a target. As a matter of fact, he enjoyed a good press in the major English-language newspapers, but a relatively poor one in the Italian sheets.

The error in identification, however, in no way slowed Petrosino's work. In the meantime, his investigation had by sheer chance crossed another that was being conducted by William J. Flynn, a Secret Service agent, in connection with a gang of Italian counterfeiters operating in New Orleans, Pittsburgh, and New York. This gang was accustomed to hold its business meetings at the Star of Italy. Hence it was quite likely that the two investigators were on the trail of the same persons.

Partly as a result of the information supplied by Flynn, Giuseppe Petrosino narrowed his own suspicions to a group of eight men. Their names should be remembered because they will reappear frequently as this story develops. They were:

Giuseppe Morello, born in Corleone, who was generally believed to be the chief of the Black Hand in New York;

Ignazio Lupo, known as "The Wolf" (from his surname), a man of some education (he had also worked as a bookseller for some time) but feared because of his violence, and specializing chiefly in extortion;

Giuseppe Fontana, who was formally accused in Italy of having murdered Marquis Emanuele di Notarbartolo, a director of the Bank of Sicily, on orders from "the king of the Mafia," Raffaele Palizzolo, a deputy from Palermo to the Italian Parliament;

Tommaso Petto, known as "The Bull" because of his remarkable physique, which had won him titles in a number of male beauty contests. Petto, who said he was a presser by trade, was actually a professional killer;

Vito Cascio Ferro, a "man of respect" who had only recently arrived in New York from Sicily; and, finally,

Giuseppe Favaro, Vito Lo Baido and Antonio Genova, known for their sordid pasts and for their connection with Morello in a blood oath.

All these men were Sicilians and all were engaged in counterfeiting operations.

Proceeding with their investigations, the two detectives concluded that "the man in the barrel," too, must have been connected in some way with the criminal activities of Giuseppe Morello and friends. But how were they to prove this? Again it was Flynn who found the right track. Some time earlier, in Pittsburgh, the Secret Service man had arrested a counterfeiter named Giuseppe Di Primo who was now serving a sentence in Sing Sing.

"Di Primo," Flynn told Petrosino, "was working for Morello, and now he'll be anxious for revenge on his accomplices because they've left him in a mess. Who knows? Maybe you can manage to get something out of him since you speak Italian."

A day later Petrosino was talking with Di Primo in the visitors' room at Sing Sing. "Do you know this man?" the detective asked, producing a photograph of the murder victim.

"Why, that's Nitto!" Di Primo exclaimed. "That's my brother-in-law, Benedetto Madonnia, who lives in Buffalo with my sister. But he looks like a dead man in the picture! What's happened to him? Has he been sick?"

Petrosino did not answer this question. "Could you tell me when and why he went to New York?"

"I sent him," Di Primo said. "He had come to see me and I asked him to go and pick up certain things belonging to me from Giuseppe Morello. But please," he insisted, "tell me what's happened to him. Is he sick?"

"He's not sick. He's dead. He's been murdered," the detective replied, thinking perhaps that the sudden shock might make the man talk.

What happened, however, was the opposite. Di Primo would not answer any further questions. "This is something I'll take care of on my own as soon as I'm out," he said with finality.

None the less, Petrosino went back quite satisfied to police headquarters. Obviously Benedetto Madonnia had gone to collect his brother-in-law's money from Morello. Perhaps he had also resorted to threats, and Morello had had him killed.

That same evening Inspector McCafferty was ordered to make a dragnet raid at the Star of Italy. The whole gang was picked up. Except for Tommaso Petto, who put up such a fight that it required four policemen to subdue him, there was no resistance; the others' experience of American laws had made them optimists.

Thorough searches ordered by Inspector McCafferty showed that all eight men were armed with pistols and knives. In Tommaso Petto's pocket there was also a pawn ticket for a watch.

Meanwhile Giuseppe Morello and Vito Cascio Ferro, who seemed to be the "brains" of the gang, had not wasted any time. Having sent for their attorney, Le Barbier, one of the best known criminal lawyers in New York, they applied to be released on bail. The request was perfectly proper, and the court was reluctantly compelled to grant it. But the court set what was for those days very high sums, in the hope that the gangsters would not be able to raise enough money.

Bond was set at five thousand dollars for Morello, the same amount for Lupo, three thousand for Petto, two thousand for Favaro, one thousand for Cascio Ferro and five hundred dollars for each of the others. The total came to sixteen thousand dollars, a huge amount at that time. The court's hopes, however, were dashed by the efficiency of the Sicilian underworld. The next morning Le Barbier appeared in court with a barber named Macaluso from Mott Street. Macaluso had a large handkerchief in which was wrapped the entire sum needed to release all eight gangsters on bail.

"This money," the lawyer lost no time in informing the court, in order to stave off any investigation of its sources, "comes from a collection taken up in the Italian quarter."

A few hours later, Morello and his associates left their cells and were hailed in the street by a little crowd made up of their friends and relatives.

Still trembling with rage, Police Commissioner William McAdoo* summoned his best detectives to a conference on the problem. Petrosino, who was among them, took his usual advantage of the opportunity to denounce the stupidity of the American laws that enabled criminals to make fools of the police. "With Italian crimi-

---

*Later Secretary of the Treasury and son-in-law of President Woodrow Wilson.—Translator.

nals you have to use Italian methods," he concluded, "otherwise America will always go on being a playground for them."

McAdoo calmed him with a gesture. "You know very well that our Constitution is inviolable. We have to protect our society through our laws."

Petrosino shrugged resentfully. "At least give me a team of Italians," he said. "With Irishmen and Jews you'll never get a spider out of its web."

"You are well aware that your request is under study by the Board of Alderman," McAdoo retorted.

"I know; for two years," Petrosino snorted. "And in the meantime Italians' applications to join the police force go on being turned down. But do you realize," he went on, raising his voice, "that in this city, which has a half-million Italians, the number of policemen who can speak their language is exactly eleven, including myself and Bonoil, who is really French and Irish?"

"You're right, Petrosino, you're right," McAdoo soothed him. "I'm doing everything I can, you know that—"

"I know, Commissioner, I know," the detective agreed. "But things can't go on this way. I spend my life arresting people and then for one reason or another the courts turn them loose."

"All right," McAdoo said, "let's get back to what we were talking about. The investigation will be begun again from scratch. More evidence is needed to make it possible to keep those gangsters securly in jail. It's my opinion that Petrosino ought to go to Buffalo tomorrow and talk to the Madonnia family. Maybe he'll be able to pick up some new clues."

Everyone agreed. Petrosino asked McCafferty to let him have the watch that the police had redeemed with the pawn ticket found on Tommaso Petto. "Even this might turn out to be evidence," he remarked, looking at the cheap, thick Roskoff that McCafferty handed him.

Petrosino's hunch turned out to be good. The watch had indeed belonged to Benedetto Madonnia, and his wife and son identified it at once.

The woman explained further that it was she who had written

the note found in the murdered man's pocket. A friend had warned
her that Nitto was in serious danger in New York and she had
written to him to persuade him to come back home.

As a result of the information supplied by the victim's relatives,
Joseph Petrosino was finally able to reconstruct the whole pattern
of the affair. After his own arrest, Giuseppe Di Primo had sent his
brother-in-law, Benedetto Madonnia, to Giuseppe Morello to collect Di Primo's share of the proceeds from the sale of an issue of
counterfeit money. Morello, however, had refused, and, after a
heated argument, Madonnia had threatened to go to the police.

That had amounted to signing his own death warrant. The actual
murder was committed by Tommaso Petto, the gang's killer. Of
this Petrosino was absolutely certain. In addition to having found
the pawn ticket in Petto's possession, the detective had learned from
some of the customers of the Star of Italy that Madonnia and Petto
had left the bar together on the evening of the murder.

Satisfied with his trip to Buffalo, Petrosino took the first train
back to New York. He was in a hurry. Now that he finally had in
his hands the evidence that would back Tommaso Petto up against
the wall, he did not want to lose any time lest the gang manage
to disappear.

But when the detective reached headquarters he got a nasty
surprise: *The New York Evening Journal* had come out a few
hours earlier with an exclusive story on the Madonnia family's
identification of the watch.

"By now they'll all be gone," Petrosino said angrily, throwing
down the newspaper. But he was wrong.

Improbably, that night policemen of the Second District managed
to round up almost the entire gang. They found its members sitting
quietly in the Star of Italy, drinking wine and playing cards. The
only missing member was Vito Cascio Ferro, and Schmittberger
was able to establish that he had fled to New Orleans. In his report Schmittberger pointed out that, in contrast to his habitual behavior, Tommaso Petto had submitted to arrest without offering
any resistance.

It should be pointed out here that this exemplary behavior by

Petto and the rest of the gang had a special reason. On the advice of Vito Cascio Ferro, the gangsters had replaced Petto with a double: another man whose complexion, moustache and unusual physique matched those of The Bull. This man was born Giovanni Carlo Costantino, but in America, to which he had come only a few months before, he had changed his name to Giovanni Pecoraro. On the night of the roundup he refused to identify himself to the policemen who mistook him for Petto. All that he would say was: "I am not Petto."

By no means convinced, the police went through his pockets and found a document in the name of Tommaso Petto, twenty-four years old. "So you're not Petto?" they said, shoving the paper in front of him. The presumed Petto said nothing and submitted to arrest.

The unbelievable exchange of identities planned by the criminals was completely successful. Two days later when, in accordance with American legal practice, the accused were brought into court for arraignment, no one had yet been able to unmask the deception.

The hearing began at nine o'clock in the morning of April 29, 1903. Tommaso Petto was charged with having been the actual killer and the others were accused of having been his accessories. It should hardly be necessary to add that the whole thing turned into a farce right at the start.

The supposed Tommaso Petto, speaking through an interpreter, asked to be permitted to make a statement. When permission was granted, he said in a loud voice: "I am not Tommaso Petto!" The announcement set off a hum of surprised whispers in the courtroom.

"Then who are you?" the presiding magistrate asked.

"My name is Giovanni Pecoraro. I can prove it." Shouts and laughter rose in the courtroom, filled with Italian spectators.

"Then why didn't you say so before?" the magistrate asked.

"I told the policemen who arrested me two nights ago that I wasn't Petto," Pecoraro pointed out, giving the interpreter time to translate. "Since then I haven't had a chance to talk to anybody who speaks my language."

At the end of the hearing Giovanni Pecoraro was released, but the others were remanded for trial on charges of homicide. However, given the new turn that the case had taken and the continuing absence of the real Tommaso Petto, the charges could not be proved.

Only Giuseppe Morello and Ignazio Lupo were to go on trial: for the manufacture and sale of counterfeit money. They were convicted and sentenced to twenty-five years' imprisonment, but, because of their lawyers' skill, they succeeded in having the sentences suspended.

Giuseppe Di Primo, Benedetto Madonnia's brother-in-law, came out of Sing Sing two years later. Petrosino was at once informed that the ex-convict had been seen at the Star of Italy, where he had kept asking for news of his friend, Tommaso Petto.

"Don't interfere with him, but keep an eye on him," the detective told his men. "You can't tell; he may lead us to The Bull."

Instead, Giuseppe Di Primo managed to drop out of sight. A month later word came to New York City Police Headquarters from Wilkes-Barre, Pennsylvania, that Tommaso Petto, who in the interval had changed his name to Tom Carrillo, had been killed on his own doorstep by an unknown assailant.

"Di Primo was smarter than we were" was all that Petrosino had to say.

2. The Turn-of-the-Century Years

AT THE OPENING OF THE TWENTIETH CENTURY New York was the second biggest "Italian city"—after Naples. One-fourth of New York's population—more than a half-million of its two million people—was Italian. A million more Italians were scattered throughout the various states of the Union.

A tremendous wave of immigration, which had originated in the southernmost, poorest, parts of Italy, had poured into America within a few years, creating problems that were often insoluble. While the growing industries of America urgently needed an army of cheap workers, the country as a whole was absolutely unprepared for their arrival. In consequence, the first contacts between the Italians and the New World were extremely harsh. Lacking schooling; rendered blind, deaf and dumb by their inability to express themselves in the language of the country, the immigrants wound up clinging together, so that in every city they formed a ghetto in which they lived under conditions that it is difficult to describe.

In New York, for instance, the half-million Italians who had decided to stay in the city were crammed into the crumbling wooden houses of the Lower East Side, beneath the Brooklyn Bridge, which earlier immigrants to New York had long since abandoned in favor of new homes in more modern residential areas. The Italians' settlement of the Lower East Side, of course, made fortunes for speculators and landlords, but also it transformed the neighborhood into a kind of human antheap in which suffering, crime, ignorance and filth were the dominant elements.

Reports by authoritative observers who studied living conditions in the area at that time present a chilling picture of the situation. Giuseppe Giacosa, an Italian playwright who visited the East Side in 1898, wrote: "It is impossible to depict the degradation, the dirt, the squalor, the stinking muck, the rubble, the disorder of the neighborhood."

Such was the Italian quarter of New York at the turn of the century—an agglomeration of varied regional groups where every day was the feast day of some patron saint, in which the streets rang with shouts in every dialect of Italy, but in which a word of English was almost never spoken. An anthill in constant movement, where pedestrians had always to be on the alert to dodge the showers of slops that poured down from windows, where more than five thousand pushcarts clogged the streets, selling everything from shoelaces to sausages.

This was the environment to which hundreds of thousands of Italians had immigrated and in which now they battled to make new lives for themselves. Forgotten by their government, which confined itself to rejoicing in the substantial income provided by the "policy of exporting labor," scorned by the aristocrats in the diplomatic service who were almost ashamed to be the representatives of such a horde, they soon found themselves once more, as they had been in the country they had left, at the mercy of speculators and criminals.

It goes without saying that the teeming Italian quarter created a major problem for the police almost from the start. Hundreds of criminals, gleefully landing in America through the careless system of issuing passports set up by the Italian government for the purpose of ridding itself not only of the hungry but also of the deviant, found this section the ideal soil in which to transplant their own Mafia-like methods.

Detective Joseph Petrosino, who was at that time the best-known Italian in New York, struggled fiercely to stem the flow of criminals that was threatening to contaminate irremediably the growing Italian colony. But his efforts were in vain. Liberal American laws and traditions did not afford the means required for the thorough execution of a cleanup program. As a result the American authorities eventually became resigned to the idea that Little Italy would turn into a plague spot. They contented themselves with symbolically enclosing the Italian ghetto inside a *cordon sanitaire,* leaving the minority of criminals free, or virtually free, to levy tribute on the vast majority of their compatriots. In short, let the Italians straighten things out for themselves; what mattered was to keep them from overflowing into the better parts of the city.

A symptom of this almost fatalistic acquiescence in the Italian problem was to be found in a report by the Police Commissioner of the time, William McAdoo. He wrote:

In view of the frightening crowding of the population, the large number of families that every tenement contains, the conditions of the neighborhoods and the narrowness of the streets, the Lower East Side, where the Italians live, represents an insoluble problem for the police.

The density of population in some areas verges on the unbelievable. It is simply impossible to pack human beings into these honeycombs towering over the narrow canyons of streets and then propose to turn them into citizens who respect and obey the laws.

Moreover, the law itself did everything it could to forfeit all respect. The Italian immigrants found a prevailingly hostile climate in America. Often they were forced to suffer the outrages of Irish gangsters under the scornful watch of policemen who were also

Irish. Indeed, the New York City police force was composed almost entirely of Irishmen and Jews—in other words, of representatives of the dominant ethnic groups. Of thirty thousand policemen, as Petrosino frequently pointed out, only eleven understood Italian, which was the language spoken by almost a quarter of the city's population. It was predictable, then, that the immigrants, already suspicious by tradition of any dealings with police, should have been still more distrustful of a police force that did not even understand them when they spoke. It was precisely this absence of "dialogue"—in the literal sense—between immigrants and policemen that was to help the growth of the Mafia.

In this connection it has been said that, given the aloof attitude with which America received the Italians, only the saints among them could have resisted the temptation to become gangsters or friends of gangsters. Undoubtedly this is an exaggeration, although it is not without some foundation. On the other hand, such statements serve only to lend credence to the legend according to which the Mafia gained a foothold in America because it succeeded in filling the gap created by the absence of laws and of men who knew how to compel respect for them. The truth is quite different: the Mafiosi were no reincarnations of Robin Hood but, rather, unprincipled scoundrels who preyed mercilessly on their own compatriots and scrupulously avoided irritating people who belonged to the dominant ethnic groups.

The often sensational eruptions of these cesspools of Italian criminality naturally served to augment the suspicion and antagonism with which Americans viewed the new arrivals. Public opinion, with its pattern of generalizing, very soon came to regard all Italians without exception as potential enemies or, at the very least, as people to be kept at a prudent distance. It was, indeed, in this period that America was filled with the image of the dark, small Italian, of uncertain origins, destined for the most menial employment, and quick to pull a knife.

It was in these same years—the last decade of the nineteenth century—that the curiosity of American readers was roused by newspaper use of such mysterious and untranslatable terms as *Mafia,*

Camorra, and *omertà.** One newspaper man did try to provide his readers with etymological explanations of these new terms coming into common usage. We learn from an issue of the *New York Herald* in 1891 that *omertà* is derived from *uomo* (*man*) and that it means *manliness, behaving like a man;* while Camorra comes from the Spanish (in which it means *quarrel,* whence *camorrista, a quarrelsome man*). But, while these two derivations are well founded, the origin that the same man suggested, however, for *Mafia* (which comes from the Arabic) is absolutely fantastic. He actually represents the Mafia as being the decayed heir to a patriotic organization that supposedly derived its own name from the initials of the battle cry of revolt—"*Morte Ai Francesi Italia Anela* (Death to the French; Italy is drained!)"—of the Sicilians at the time of the Sicilian Vespers in 1282.**

In any event, the word *Mafia* first appeared in major American newspapers in March of 1891 in connection with the "New Orleans lynching," a tragic business that cost the lives of eleven Italians. The event, which created a great stir throughout the world and led to a virtual threat of war by Italy, was brought on by an incident of typical Mafia character. At that time a large Sicilian colony had taken root in Louisiana, where the immigrants had found a physical environment much like that of their native island and had established many farms devoted to the cultivation of vegetables and citrus fruits.

Unfortunately, as was always the case in those years, not only thousands of industrious Sicilian farm workers but also some twenty criminals had come ashore at New Orleans, and the latter had set up a profitable extortion industry. This crowd, dominated by the Provenzano family and known also as the Stoppers, had exercised

---

*The traditional dialect term that still survives in New York criminal circles for the obligation of silence in any dealings with the authorities; an obligation that extends even to victims.—Translator.

**The riot that began at vespers in a Palermo church on Easter Monday, 30 March, and turned into a massacre of the French was the start of the revolt by the Sicilians against Charles I, the Angevin dynasty's first King of the Two Sicilies (Sicily and Naples, the latter being the kings' preferred seat).—Translator.

unchallenged control of the city's fruit and vegetable market until a second gang had gone into action. This one was ruled by the Matranga family and was called the Gardeners. It too had begun to prey on the growers and thus to thrust itself into what the Stoppers regarded as their territory.

The two gangs came into conflict. There ensued a kind of small war in which half a dozen died, but the local authorities, observing that it was only a matter of trouble between Italians, did not give it too much attention.

The citizenry, however, was prompt to anger when the chief of police, Dave Hennessey, was killed. Found mortally wounded on the night of October 18, 1890, he still had time to say before he died: "It was the dagoes, the Italians." And that was enough to set off the pogrom.

New Orleans, a city well known then chiefly for its brothels and its gambling houses, was not a community of saints. Violence was the normal way of business. Nevertheless, the horrendous crime committed by Italians against a member of the ruling class set off a kind of holy war.

But the crusader spirit that seized the residents of one of the most turbulent cities in the United States merely explains the bloody conclusion of the affair. It is rather rewarding to explore briefly the biography of the murdered man, inasmuch as he has gained a place in his country's history as *the first American victim of the Italian Mafia.*

Dave Hennessey came from that sort of wild Irish background that, until the rise of the Italian gangsters, supplied most of the criminals and adventurers that roamed America. The son of a soldier of fortune killed in a bar-room brawl, Hennessey had roamed the west for a long time, living sometimes as an outlaw and sometimes as a collector of bounties on other outlaws. He had also been tried for two murders, but was acquitted both times. Later he had settled in New Orleans, where one of his cousins, formerly chief of police, had been dismissed for improper conduct. Dave managed to get himself elected to the same post. He also joined the Red Lantern Club, the social purposes of which may be inferred from the fact that that kind of lantern was used then to identify whorehouses.

In any case, Hennessey proved to be the tough, firm policeman that his supporters wanted. A few months before his death, for example, he had succeeded in capturing a famous Calabrian bandit, one Giovanni Esposito, who was wanted in Italy for eighteen murders and also for the kidnapping of the English Protestant minister, Godwin Rose, one of whose ears the bandit cut off and sent to Mrs. Rose by way of proving that it was her husband whom he held. At the same time, it ought to be pointed out that Chief Hennessey was a man by no means impervious to corruption. In this connection it was known that during the previous year he had saved a number of members of the Provenzano gang, on trial for murder, by giving testimony that was, to say the least, shocking.

His murder, however, aroused the greatest indignation; and it was the occasion for an American newspaper's first mention of the name of one Joseph Petrosino, a New York policeman, whom they described as an expert on Italian matters. Indeed, Petrosino was asked his opinion of the murder; he replied that the New Orleans investigators would be well advised to look into "the victim's past," by which he meant the possibility of collusion between the murdered man and members of the Mafia.

This was, in fact, the right direction. It was then discovered that Dave Hennessey had had a number of "warnings" from the Matrangas, who accused him of systematically taking the other gang's side. But the evidence that the chief of police had allowed himself to be bought by the Provenzanos did not in the slightest dilute the general grief over his demise, even though it tended to show that it was the Matrangas' Gardeners who had killed Hennessey.

The seventeen members of the gang were all arrested. They were Carlo Matranga, Antonio Scaffidi, Antonio Bagnetto, Emanuele Polizzi, Antonio Marchese, his fourteen-year-old son Aspero, Pietro Monastero, Bastiano Incardona, Salvatore Sunseri, Carlo Trajna, James Caruso, Rocco Geraci and Charles Patorno—all Sicilians— as well as Lorenzo Comitez, Charles Poitza, J. P. Macheca and

Frank Romero, whose exact places of origin could not be established but all of whom, in spite of their names, were also Italians.

All those arrested denied the charges. Only Emanuele Polizzi,
who was to be found of unsound mind, signed a jumbled confession that he later recanted.

In any event, the residents of New Orleans were unanimously
convinced of their guilt. Two bodies were established for the
occasion: a Council of Fifty, made up of influential citizens, and a
Vigilance Committee whose task it was to make certain that
justice was done. Secret organizations also entered the affair—
groups such as the Ku Klux Klan and the White League, which,
as they had done before against the blacks, began now to harass
the Italians with the aim of "safeguarding racial purity."

Very difficult days ensued for the sixty thousand Sicilian farm
workers in the Louisiana fields. Bands of masked horsemen, the
so-called night riders, ransacked and burned many of the farms.
Fiery crosses appears on hillsides and many crops were destroyed.

The surge of hatred reached new peaks. Two thousand Sicilians
who arrived at this time at New Orleans without the slightest fore-
knowledge of what had happened were welcomed by a howling
mob hurling rocks at them. Another indication of the mounting
violence was the act of a certain Thomas Duffy. He went to the
city jail and asked to speak with one of the suspects, Antonio
Scaffidi, whom he had never seen before. Then, when the Sicilian
was brought to him, Duffy put a pistol bullet into his neck. For
this Duffy was sentenced to six months' imprisonment.

Whether they were innocent or guilty, the Gardeners were
meanwhile preparing for their trial, for which they had retained
the best lawyers in the state. Money was not one of their problems;
it seems that the *friends** scattered throughout the country sent them
about seventy-five thousand dollars.

Furthermore the trial gave no sign of being a problem for them
either. Except for Polizzi's repudiated confession, no concrete evidence against them had been found.

---

*A traditional Mafia euphemism for Mafia members. It is often called "the
friendly society."—Translator.

The courtroom sessions dragged on for several days, while groups of troublemakers demonstrated outside. But finally, on March 13, 1891, all the defendants except three—Scaffidi, Polizzi and Monastero—were acquitted.

As was to be expected, the verdict set off a new surge of resentment. The jurors were accused (apparently with cause) of having been bought off, and some of them were manhandled by the crowd. The defense lawyers too were attacked, and they had to leave town.

But the worst was still to come.

The city's revenge was organized in official fashion. The mayor, whose name was Shakespeare and whose performance at this time later helped him to be elected governor of the state, called the citizenry to a mass meeting. A proclamation was distributed; its last sentence was: "Come prepared for action!" The local newspapers printed articles that were outright incitements to lynching. As for the Vigilance Committee, it distributed weapons to the more daring.

On the morning of March 14 a crowd of about six thousand persons gathered in a public square. From an improvised platform a lawyer named W. S. Parkerson harangued them. "Are there men here," he cried, "who have the courage to render justice where that vile jury has failed?"

"Yes!" the mob shouted back. "Let's go get the Italians and hang them all."

To howl was to act. The mob set out for the prison, screaming: "Give us the dagoes!"

The dagoes—the Italians—who had not yet been released, asked the prison warden, John Davis, to help them, but he threw up his hands and said there was nothing he could do. He knew that the mob would not stop at the jail gate. Nevertheless, when he heard the outer door being knocked down by the mob, Davis took the Italians out of their cells and urged them to hide wherever they could.

As soon as the armed mob had broken into the jail it began the manhunt. Six of the seventeen Italians succeeded in finding refuge in the women's division. It was filled with prostitutes, some of whom unselfishly concealed the men beneath their full skirts. The others were captured one by one.

J. P. Macheca was shot to death as he tried to defend himself with a tomahawk that he had somehow obtained. Bagnetto was snatched off the floor where he had thrown himself down, feigning death. Polizzi was dragged out of a dog's kennel; Scaffidi was found behind a pile of garbage; Natali was pulled from a heap of dirty clothes. Antonio Marchese was taken out of the death cell in which he had hidden, and his fourteen-year-old son, Aspero, was picked up in the prison yard; he was not killed.

Later the prisoners were hanged from the trees of Treme Street. The branch broke to which Bagnetto's rope was looped, but a youth ran up at once and fastened the rope over a stronger branch. Then, as the victims gyrated in their death agonies, thirty "picked sharp-shooters" of the Vigilance Committee emptied the magazines of their Winchesters into the dying bodies.

After the butchery, while throngs of excited women were bathing their handkerchiefs in the Italians' blood or tearing pieces from their clothing to keep as trophies, Parkerson addressed the mob again. "Now justice has been done," he said. "If I need you again, I will call on you. Go back quietly to your homes. God bless you all!"

"And God bless you, Mr. Parkerson," the mob shouted back. Men lifted the lawyer to their shoulders and bore him in triumph to his residence.

The events of New Orleans stirred the whole world to horror. With the exception of a few newspapers in the south, the American press joined the European in denunciation of the savagery. *The Times* of London said: "Italy's anger is shared by the entire civilized world." The Italian government, which was headed at the time by Marchese Antonio Starabba di Rudinì, a Sicilian, took drastic measures: it went to the extreme of recalling its ambassador from Washington and initiating a *de facto* rupture of diplomatic relations. There was even some demand for a declaration of war, and such a possibility was taken seriously by many people even in America. Panic flared in New Orleans, for example, when a newspaper reported that the Italian fleet was making for the Louisiana coast in order to shell the city. The story was sheer fantasy, of course, but in some circles in Washington the fear was expressed that the Italian navy, with twenty-two fighting ships, might attack the American coast. A Democratic paper, *The Times-Democrat*, stated at this time that the United States, with only one battleship, which, futhermore, was not even completed, was virtually "at the mercy of the Italian warships." And it is interesting to recall that on this very pretext the American government announced a new bond issue at this period for the development of the fleet, thus initiating the growth of the American navy.

The dispute with Italy was settled in the following year, when President Harrison offered, by way of renewing ties with Italy, to pay an indemnity of one hundred twenty-five thousand lire to the family of each victim. Rudinì accepted the offer at once, but the attempt at placation cost Harrison heavily. In fact the Democrats succeeded in unseating him in the next Presidential election, accusing him of having "used taxpayers' money to pay off the murderers of Dave Hennessey."

The eleven men hanged in New Orleans, unfortunately, were not the only Italians to fall victim to what is known as Lynch Law. The historical section of the Italian Foreign Ministry still has hundreds of folders dealing with lynchings of Italians in the United States. For instance:

1895: three Italians were lynched in Walsemburg, Colorado, after they had been acquitted of a homicide charge;

1896: in Hanville, Louisiana, three Sicilians accused of murder were taken from the jail in which they were being held for trial and were hanged in the public square;

1899: in Tallulah, Louisiana, five Italians—Francesco, Carlo and Giuseppe Difatta, brothers, and their friends, Giovanni Cerani and Rosario Fiducia, all from Cefalù, Sicily—were lynched after a bloodless quarrel with a certain Dr. Hodges who objected when the Sicilians' goats strayed onto his land.

These were the more notorious cases, but the list could go much farther. Furthermore, the victims were not always criminals, convicted or accused. In many cases they were simply immigrants who had been reduced to tramping through the country; in others they were men who, having endured violence at the hands of their compatriots in the "Italian quarters" of various large cities, had gone off to the interior of the country in the hope merely of finding a plot of land on which they could live in peace.

In New York no Italian was ever lynched. But the reason is to be sought in the fact that the Italian colony lived in virtual isolation. Locked into their own ghetto, the immigrants lived their lives in the unaltered preservation of their respective regional traditions, continuing to talk in their old dialects and often dying without having ever had contact with the American society that was evolving only a few blocks from them.

In this climate the Mafia, as a criminal organization capable of controlling every kind of activity, was to develop later. But in the turn-of-the-century years the criminals who arrived in New York from Italy, even though they had all the characteristics of the Mafioso, were absolutely unequipped to bring into being a real industry of crime. Moreover, these individuals were predominantly sheep, whose unshakable ignorance was matched only by their cruelty.

As a result, the earliest Mafia organizations that operated in New York were given to primitive and ruthless methods. In one way and another they established criminal bands, more or less interconnected, the sole purpose of which was to prey upon their own compatriots.

The immigrants, who landed in New York with only the fifty lire required for their papers, fell into criminal clutches the moment they set foot on the pier. Steered into dubious employment agencies, they were then hired by various firms that subjected them to the sweatshop system—maximum hours, minimum pay. Furthermore, a large part of their miserable wages was siphoned off by various "deductions." The rare man who managed, nonetheless, to save a few dollars always wound up entrusting them to some "banker" who unfailingly stole him bare.

The criminals who managed to spread terror outside the Italian sector of New York as well as within it were those of the so-called Black Hand. In a few years this frightening name acquired such magic that often the mark of a coal-blackened hand pressed against a house door was sufficient to make a family leave town.

It is much to be doubted, however, whether the Black Hand was a real "society," a solid organization with sophisticated ramifications like the Cosa Nostra of the present. Even though everyone pointed to Joseph Petrosino as the number one enemy of the Black Hand, he rejected the notion for years. He contended that small groups of criminals, and even some operating individually, had adopted this symbol of terror precisely because everyone was frightened of it.

What is more, the Black Hand was not the invention of Sicilian criminals. The name was that of a secret society founded by Spanish anarchists that spread later to other countries, particularly in the Balkans, with the purpose of assassinating monarchs and other chiefs of state.

Hence it is quite probable that the symbol of the Black Hand was introduced into America by European anarchists. The fact remains, however, that the Italian criminals took it over to further their various ends.

Toward the end of the nineteenth century, in fact, the Italian section of New York experienced a sudden flood of extortion letters bearing the print of a hand and bordered with designs of skulls and crossed daggers. No immigrant who had risen to a certain level of prosperity escaped these letters. The victim was given an ultimatum to place a certain sum of money at a given point. Those who did not pay were killed or their businesses or houses were dynamited.

The perpetrators relied, of course, on the victims' *omertà,* and in any event resort to the police would only have made for worse reprisals. On the other hand, very soon every crime committed in the Italian section was indiscriminantly ascribed to the Black Hand, and this generalization, besides aggravating distrust of the Italian community, was enormously useful to the underworld. Even the most stubborn skeptics were finally convinced of the existence of a secret society endowed with great powers and a large membership. And, in the end, everyone gave in to the rule of *pay or die.*

As the exception that proves the rule, let me quote a letter that appeared at this period in *The New York Times:*

My name is Salvatore Spinelli. My parents in Italy came from a decent family. I came here eighteen years ago and went to work as a house painter, like my father. I started a family and I have been an American citizen for thirteen years. My children all went to school as soon as they were old enough. I went into business. I began to think I was doing well. Everybody in my family was happy. I had a house at 314 East Eleventh Street and another one at 316, which I rented out. At this point the "Black Hand" came into my life and asked me for seven thousand dollars. I told them to go to hell and the bandits tried to blow up my house. Then I asked the police for help and refused more demands, but the "Black Hand" set off one, two, three, four, five bombs in my houses. Things went to pieces. From thirty-two tenants I am down to six. I owe a thousand dollars in interest that is due next month and I cannot pay. I am a ruined man. My family lives in fear. There is a policeman on guard in front of my house, but but what can he do? My brother Francesco and I do guard duty at the windows with guns night and day. My wife and children have not left the house for weeks. How long is all this going to go on?

3. The Black Hand: From Myth to Reality

THE "BARREL MURDER" marked an important date in the career of Detective Joseph Petrosino. He could not have known, of course, that one of the men arrested in that case would kill him six years later in the darkness of a square in Palermo. At the same time, the intuition of a veteran policeman kept him particularly on guard against these men, who seemed far more cunning than those with whom he was accustomed to dealing. Apparently something was changing in the world of American crime. Perhaps a new generation of criminals was coming to maturity.

In addition, the cleverness that the Morello gang had shown in organizing its own defense had thrown everyone off balance. The device, for example, of replacing one of its members with a double who had only just arrived from Sicily and who was therefore a novice in these surroundings attested to the operation of an organizing intelligence and ramifications never before suspected.

In spite of this new experience, Petrosino would still not have refused to repeat what he had said on April 14 and on earlier occasions about the "myth" of the Black Hand. One such statement appeared in the *Herald* of February 20, 1903.

"There is only one thing that can wipe out the Black Hand," the detective said, "and that is the elimination of ignorance. The gangsters who are holding Little Italy in the grip of terror come chiefly from Sicily and southern Italy, and they are primitive country robbers transplanted to the cities. This is proved by their brutal methods. No American hold-up man would ever think of stopping somebody and slashing his face with a knife just to take his wallet. Probably he would simply threaten him with a pistol. No American criminal would blow up a man's house or kill his children just because he refused to pay fifty or a hundred dollars.

"The crimes that occur among the Italians here," Petrosino continued, "are the same as those committed at one time by rural outlaws in Italy; and the victims, like the killers, come from the same ignorant class of people. In short, we are dealing with rural banditry transplanted to the most modern city in the world."

At this point a reporter asked him: "How do you propose to solve the crime problem among your compatriots?"

"If a Vigilance Committee is formed in the Italian colony," the detective replied, "and if the prosperous Italians will take the trouble to educate the ignorant and convince them that American laws exist for their protection too, the problem will solve itself. There is nothing invincible about the so-called members of the Black Hand, and the day will come, I hope, when we will begin to find some of them hanging from lamp-posts or cut to pieces in the streets."

"Do you want to reach the point of lynching?" the reporter asked.

"No. All I want is justice," Petrosino replied.

In actuality Joseph Petrosino would not have hesitated to slash to ribbons any one of the countless cutthroats who flourished in the alleys of the Lower East Side. The man was hot-blooded and violent. The endless frustration of seeing the courts promptly release men whom he had arduously hunted down had made him hard and pitiless. The gangsters who had had dealings with him bore marks of the "interrogation" for months; especially when he realized that the evidence in his hands would not be sufficient grounds for an indictment or a deportation, he never boggled at attacking them physically. "This way you'll remember who Petrosino is," he would remind them after he had finished beating them.

He also did everything he could to make life difficult for them in New York; he arrested them whenever possible, he harassed their friends and customers, until the criminals finally found themselves completely cut off and so shifted their operations to more tolerant regions. "I've gotten rid of more criminals this way than with the help of the courts," he told his colleagues.

The frenetic zeal of Petrosino, the only detective in the whole of New York City who could understand Italian, resulted, however, in no let-up in the output of what were called "knife letters." By 1904 the problem of the Black Hand—whether myth or concrete organization—had attained national importance; it was discussed at the governmental level, both state and federal; but no one gave any thought to Petrosino's persistent requests for the creation of an Italian-speaking police squad. The authorities in New York, in fact, still tended to discriminate against Italians. Petrosino was an exception; the rest . . . well, better to keep them out. And not only out of the white-collar jobs but also out of reach of the modicum of social advancement that might be represented by a police uniform.

Meanwhile the Italian detective kept on insisting that the "Black Hand" was a fake initiated by individual criminals or separate gangs and given seeming substance by newspapermen's imaginations. Of this he had no doubt. In this same year of 1904, when the threatening letter-writers and the bomb-throwers were more active than ever before, he had a clash with Police Commissioner William McAdoo.

After he had presented his view in an official report, Petrosino went to his superior's office to stress the need to set up an Italian-speaking squad. "The Italians in New York," he said, "will never cooperate with policemen who don't even understand their language."

"I don't think they'll cooperate with anybody," the commissioner retorted. "From what I hear, the police in Sicily run up against the same obstacles."

"We aren't in Sicily here," Petrosino insisted. "And not all the Italians in New York are Sicilians. If you want to be trusted, you have to trust."

McAdoo did not agree. "I don't think the Italians deserve to be trusted," he argued. "No doubt most of them are honest people, and excellent workers, but the fact remains that they behave as if they were in enemy territory."

"Probably they are," Petrosino replied. "Do you know what my compatriots say when they talk about America? They say: 'An Italian discovered it and the Jews and the Irish run it.' Try giving the Italians a little power too, and maybe there will be some change."

The conversation ended as it generally did: McAdoo offered vague assurances and Petrosino went away completely dissatisfied. A few days later the detective again took the offensive, this time with a press conference.

"The 'Black Hand,'" he told the reporters, "is not even a group of Italian origin. Other ethnic groups used this symbol right here in New York before the Italians did, and I can give you plenty of proof. What is needed to free Little Italy from this scourge, however, is policemen who know Italian. Then the 'Black Hand' will disappear, because we are not dealing here with a real, existing criminal organization like the Mafia and the Camorra but with isolated individuals who will be accused by the victims themselves as soon as they find that they are in fact protected by the police."

Shrewdly, Joseph Petrosino teased the reporters' curiosity by showing them a bundle of extortion letters ascribed to the Black Hand.

"Take a good look at these letters," he said. "Even if you don't know Italian, you can easily observe that they're all in different handwritings. I have examined them closely, and I can state flatly that they were written not only by different people but also by people who come from different regions."

The detective strongly emphasized this point and urged the reporters also to compare the Black Hand symbols drawn at the bottom of each letter. These were indeed very varied in design: in some the hand was shown open, in others clenched into a fist, in still others pierced by a dagger or surrounded by swords and skulls.

"I think that, if we were really dealing with a single organization," Petrosino concluded, "the symbol too would be a single one." This was a logical argument and the reporters accepted it. It set off a press campaign designed to reassess the myth of the Black Hand.

A handful of newspaper articles, in any event, was not enough to alter the situation. Quite the contrary: the extortionists improved their methods, and the "knife letters" continued to frighten the selected victims with unbroken regularity. Petrosino, meanwhile, never missed an opportunity to press his ideas, even though in his own mind he was beginning to entertain certain doubts. But it was a reporter's question that brought him to crisis.

"Since, in your view, these are all cases of individual operators," the interviewer asked him, "please explain why those who agree to pay money are not bothered any more."

This was a logical question. And, embarrassed, Petrosino replied that the weakness of the police had probably made it possible for the criminals to organize themselves into more homogeneous groups. But he himself was not persuaded by this explanation. For some time he had found himself kept awake by the fear that there might indeed exist in New York a supergang with accomplices and connections at every level.

The time had come for Joseph Petrosino to reexamine his own conclusions.

In more than twenty years of police work, he had never been troubled by doubt or uncertainty. He had arrived at very specific ideas about the complex social reality in which he functioned, even if those ideas were quite limited. He had divided the people of the

world into good and evil, and he had elected to work for the good
—in other words, for the American society that had enabled him,
a newcomer, to carve out a solid, secure position for himself. Consequently all those who did not accept the rules of this system were
sinners who must be kept in line, possibly with a strong hand.

Joseph Petrosino had built his own code of behavior on these
foundations. And he was in no doubt as to the rightness of his
thinking. As a result he was ashamed of the behavior of other
Italian-Americans, behavior as to whose deep-lying causes he knew
nothing, but saw only the most visible features: crime, *omertà*,
ignorance, and inability to become part of the new social system.

On the other hand, no more could be asked of a policeman of
his cultural level. In truth, he was convinced that he was an
educated man, but only because his grade school training in a
society of illiterates made him one of the best-educated Italians in
New York.

In order to understand the noted detective's mentality, to grasp
his "Uncle Tom" complex, one must go back to the very beginning
of his story.

Giuseppe Michele Pasquale Petrosino was born in Padula, in the
Province of Salerno, on August 30, 1860. His father, Prospero,
was a tailor; his mother's maiden name was Maria Giuseppa Arato.

His parents had two other children, Caterina and Vincenzo.
Then his mother died and his father married another Padula girl,
Maria Mugno, by whom he had three more children: Antonio,
Giuseppina and Michele.

When little Giuseppe was thirteen years old, his father decided
to emigrate to America with his whole family. They departed from
Naples in the summer of 1873 in a steam-assisted sailing vessel and
arrived in New York after a voyage of twenty-five days.

Given the times, Prospero Petrosino's decision to move to America might be regarded as rather unusual. The mass emigration from
southern Italy actually began many years later. What impelled him
to leave could not have been rigorous hardship. The tailor of
Padula, while unquestionably compelled to struggle for his liveli-

hood, was not so poor as the overwhelming majority of his fellow townsmen. The fact that he had succeeded in sending his sons to elementary schools was evidence of some prosperity, however limited, for those days.

In times to come, Giuseppe (who would become Joseph) Petrosino was to pride himself on his ability to read and write; he was also to edit certain details of his biography in order to set himself ever more apart from his compatriots. When he became famous he was to tell the press that he had studied the harp and then the violin in Naples. He was lying, of course. All that is certain is that he did have a great love for music (the only diversion that he allowed himself was opera). Later in life he did in fact turn his attention to the violin, which he studied secretly in his bachelor apartment. But only a very few of his intimates had the privilege of hearing him play.

The reasons that led the elder Petrosino to emigrate to America, then, are not at all clear. A first wave of Italian emigration to the New World, it is true, had begun after 1870. But it was composed almost exclusively of Italians from the north-central area, all professionally or vocationally trained and also politically active, who left their native country not only for the legitimate reason of economic betterment but also because they were disappointed by the turn that events had taken after the achievement of the national unity to which they had so long aspired.

At the same time it is not really credible that Prospero Petrosino, a docile subject of the Bourbon king until a few years earlier, was part of that class. It is much more likely that he hoped to follow the example of a certain Vincenzo Giudice, who was the first resident of Padula to land in America and also the first Italian to wear the uniform of the New York City police force. (Padula, furthermore, was to supply many policemen to the various American forces.)

In New York the thirteen-year-old Guiseppe Petrosino manifested a certain enterprising character. With a boy of his own age, Pietro Jorio, he opened a combination newspaper and shoeshine

stand. It is interesting to note that the stand was set up right outside 300 Mulberry Street, then the site of the city's Police Headquarters.

In those days, when *racket* still had its original meaning of *loud
noise,* when exotic terms like *Mafia, Camorra, omertà* could not be
found in even the most up-to-date dictionaries of the English language, Italy was known in America chiefly as the fatherland of
Giuseppe Garibaldi, a kind of European George Washington to
whom, as everyone knew, President Lincoln had even offered the
command of an army during the Civil War.

Italians living in the United States at that time were looked on
with sympathy and in no way presented a problem. As a matter
of fact, there were exceedingly few of them: about twenty-five
thousand, according to a count made in 1878.

Young Petrosino grew up, then, in a climate still immune to the
prejudices that were to come later. He worked hard for several
years in his little newspaper/shoeshine stand and spent the rest of
his time studying English in classes at a night school set up by the
city for foreigners. By the time he was sixteen he knew his new
language quite well, even though he never learned to write it cor-
rectly. A year later he became an American citizen.* In the meantime he had also given up his menial work as a bootblack in favor
of a job with a stockbroker named De Luca, who had an office in
Broome Street.

The young man from Padula reached the first important land-
mark in his life, however, at the age of eighteen, when he succeeded in being hired by the City of New York. The job that he
got was that of an ordinary street cleaner (or whitewing, as the
city street cleaners were called then because of the white work
clothes that they wore); all the same, it was still the much coveted
steady job. It should also be noted that in those days the whitewings
came directly under the jurisdiction of the Police Department. Unconsciously, then, Petrosino was moving closer to his goal.

The young fellow did not linger long with broom and shovel.

---

*Derivatively, it is to be presumed, through the naturalization of his father,
since he was still a minor.—Translator.

He was bright, he was strong, and, what was most important, he spoke English. A year later he was a foreman assigned to supervise the movement of the garbage scows that carried off the collections for dumping into the ocean. His direct superior was Inspector Aleck Williams, an Irishman of mature years known as the Tsar of the Tenderloin—that is to say, the disreputable quarter where Petrosino himself worked.

Meanwhile—by now it was 1880—the first waves of southern emigration had begun to roll in on New York. These new arrivals were seen at once to be quite different from the Italians to whom Americans were accustomed. Quarrelsome, usually dirty, seemingly devoid of any desire to become part of their new surroundings, and, above all, always ready to pull knives even for trivial reasons, they at once created a major problem. The Irish police were a bit out of their depth with them. What surprised these policemen more than anything else was the fact that, instead of running to them for help, the victims seemed bent, in contrast, on protecting their persecutors.

Inspector Williams, in whose district the greatest number of Italians lived, was the most perplexed of all. He had no means of defending himself against these criminals from the latest shipments. And, since he did not know their language, he was not even in a position to keep an eye on them. It was for this reason that Aleck Williams began to observe with increasing interest the efficient Italian foreman who seemed to be so eager to cooperate with the authorities.

The motives that impelled Giuseppe Petrosino to join the police force were the subject of many legends in his lifetime. His detractors said that he had become a policeman out of hatred for the Sicilians, who had barred him from their gangs because he was from Salerno. His hagiographers argued, on the other hand, that he joined the force in order to redeem his country's honor, stained as it was by the behavior of a few scoundrels. The truth in any case is that his career began at the lowest level: he was an informer.

It was Inspector Williams himself who suggested that Petrosino start working for him in this capacity. With the prospect of formally joining the police later, the young man did not hesitate to agree. Besides, he felt that he was doing something proper and necessary; later in life he would refer with outright pride to his activity as an *auxiliary*.

Aleck Williams' "trusted agent" did his job very well. Fluent in almost every Italian dialect that was spoken in New York, extremely courageous and equally quick to size up a situation from a few overheard remarks, he proved to be a valuable asset in every police operation carried out in Italian surroundings.

Finally, on October 19, 1883, when he was twenty-three years old, Joseph Petrosino was authorized to wear a policeman's uniform. This had not been easy for him to achieve, even though he had been able to back up his application with the fact that, having now become known in the underworld, he was running increasing risks as an informer and at the same time becoming ever less useful.

Strong pressure by Inspector Williams was required to gain acceptance of Petrosino's application. In addition to the impediment of his Italian origin, the candidate suffered also from his inability to meet the physical requirements for the job; for, in spite of his two-hundred-pound weight, he was barely five feet three inches tall. Ultimately, however, his application was approved and New York acquired the shortest policeman in its history.

The first time he went out of his house in uniform, Petrosino did not receive the attention that, perhaps, he thought he should get. His compatriots made fun of him. Many of them shouted insults and obscenities at him as he passed. Strange plays on words began to be made on his unusual surname, which in various southern dialects means *parsley*. "Parsley will make the American police taste better," people said, "but indigestible they will always be."

After these early encounters the neophyte policeman, who had never been an expansive fellow, withdrew even more into himself. His work became the sole reason for his being. Adventures with women he had never had, and he never looked for them. Little by little, too, he gave up his few friends in the neighborhood, and finally he left the area itself and went to live by himself in a small bachelor apartment in the section favored by the Irish. He justified this to his family by explaining that he wanted to protect it against any possible reprisals. In actuality he was now a lone wolf and from then on even his relatives would see him only very rarely.

For several years Joseph Petrosino was a patrolman on Thirteenth Street, treated with a certain reserve by his Irish and Jewish colleagues. His departmental record shows that he was never accused of the slightest dereliction. In every situation he displayed efficiency, courage, shrewdness, and perfect knowledge of departmental regulations. In a word, and in the common phrase, he had found out where he belonged. He was a policeman by vocation: tough, strict, incorruptible. In Italy he would surely have become, and remained, one of those efficient Carabinieri sergeants who are the backbone of that service. But the more open society of the United States offered him greater satisfactions.

By 1890 Petrosino had already left the monotony of patrol duty and moved on to the investigation section, assigned to the surveillance of the Italian underworld. The Police Commissioner was then a man who was later to become President of the United States, Theodore Roosevelt. Well-bred and sophisticated (he was known as Silk Socks), Roosevelt was also very ambitious. Futhermore, the post of Police Commissioner constituted an excellent springboard for anyone who intended to go further in politics. Already on the road to success, Petrosino could also turn out to be very useful to Roosevelt by helping him to capture the sympathies of that group of Italian leaders who were beginning to constitute a certain force in elections.

For his part, Joseph Petrosino was shrewd enough to grasp the rules of the American political game. He realized at once, for example, that, since the post of Police Commissioner was (then) an elective one, the man who held it needed votes above all in order to go on to higher goals.

So this was the basis of his friendship with Teddy Roosevelt. They saw each other frequently, and the policeman never missed an opportunity to publicize the politician. In return, Roosevelt was to appoint Petrosino a sergeant of detectives before leaving for Washington and a post in the federal government. It was the first time an Italian had risen that high.

Petrosino was also very clever in immediately establishing the most cordial relations with the representatives of the major newspapers. As a good American he knew the value of publicity. It was common knowledge, for instance, that when he was about to make an important arrest he habitually and secretly notified the top reporters in advance so that they could be present for the event.

Besides, his work had picturesque aspects that greatly enhanced its interest for the press. From the beginning of his career, Joseph Petrosino had specialized in disguises. The closet in his apartment was more variously equipped than a theater's wardrobe. He knew how to pass himself off as a Sicilian laborer and work for weeks digging in the tunnels of Manhattan or on the roads. When he got back to headquarters, his hands were covered with calluses and his notebook was filled with information. Sometimes he shuffled through the streets of Little Italy as a blind beggar; sometimes he posed as a gangster; and he played many other parts.

As time went on, of course, this talent of his for disguises became well known, and the underworld grew more suspicious. It often happened that, as he wandered about the Italian section in one disguise or another, someone spotted the detective; then the vegetable peddlers would start intoning the virtues of their parsley as loud as they could. "I have good *parsley!*" they would chant. "See the beautiful *parsley!*" Then anyone who had reason to be frightened by the policeman's presence could quickly take the requisite precautions.

After his promotion to detective, which took place on July 20, 1895, Joseph Petrosino was completely relieved of all duties of secondary importance. From that day forth only unusual cases were assigned to him. He was also relieved of the obligation of wearing his uniform, and at once he replenished his private wardrobe. Thereafter he wore dark business suits, Prince Albert overcoats, and double-soled shoes (in order to look a little taller). The only style of hat he wore was the derby, always buying the highest available, again in order to look taller. Because of this unvarying taste (he rarely removed his hat, lest people see his incipient baldness), he began to be called "the detective in the derby."

Unfortunately, even dressing like a gentleman could not make Petrosino look attractive. He was a squat, heavyset man, with a peasant's round face that still showed traces of the smallpox from which as a child he had suffered in Padula. Luigi Barzini,* who knew him then, has described him:

He was a stout, strong man. His clean-shaven face was coarse-featured, and marred by light pocking; at first sight he did not attract. But in that butcher's face there was the impress of a stubborn will and of courage, something that made one think of a mastiff. There was more of the wrestler than of the policeman in Petrosino. One sensed that he was better at thrashing the evildoer than at finding him.

An American writer, on the other hand, said of him:

At first sight he looks like a man who owns a shop or a café in Little Italy. He lacks refinement and seems rather slow of comprehension. His face is expressionless, and he could move through a crowd without attracting anyone's attention. But it is precisely this that is the detective's strength. He is a master in the art of feigning a timid naivete. But more than one robber and killer have learned to their cost how quick is his mind and how nimble is his arm.

In a few years "the detective in the derby" had become famous in New York and in neighboring states. This fanatically upright Italian who fought courageously against his own dishonest compatriots aroused Americans' curiosity. Everything he did made news, as they say. One reporter compared Petrosino to one of those ultra-faithful Indian scouts who helped the American cavalry to track Apaches and Cheyennes to their hiding places. And the resemblance, with all its implications of racism, was not at all unfounded, even

---

*The bilingual author, member of the Italian Parliament.—Translator.

though Scout Petrosino was a hunter of men who were more to be dreaded than the Indians.

On the night of July 17, 1898, two policemen on patrol in Leonard Street, in that part of Manhattan where Little Italy abuts on Chinatown, heard a man's desperate screams. On the run, pistols in hand, they hurried in the direction of the cries: the corner of Baxter Street, not far from the Trinacria Café that was generally patronised by Sicilians.

When the two policemen arrived, the shouting had stopped. If anyone had been keeping watch meanwhile at a window, or at the door of the café, he had taken good care to disappear. Once more the street was plunged in darkness and silence.

Looking carefully in all directions as they advanced, guns in hand, the two policemen heard a kind of hoarse gasping that came from behind the corner of a house. As they went nearer they saw a young man who still held a bloodstained knife in his hand while he looked down in shock at another man lying flat on his face in the gutter.

The man with the knife was at once disarmed and handcuffed. There was nothing to be done for the other; he had been killed instantly by a stab in the back.

As far as the two policemen were concerned the case was open and shut. It was just one more of those fights between two Italians, and this time the killer had been caught almost in the act.

The suspect, one Angelo Carboni, twenty-five years old, was interrogated more in sign language than in words. As a matter of fact, he knew no English, and the policemen knew no Italian. It was possible, however, to determine that Carboni had had a quarrel that evening inside the Trinacria Café with a forty-two-year-old man from his native village, Natale Brogno, and they had then left the café, apparently to settle matters in the street. As far as Angelo Carboni was concerned, he admitted without hesitation that this was the case, but he stubbornly and sobbingly rejected the accusation of homicide.

"We were fighting with our fists in the dark," he later explained, "when suddenly Brogno fell down in front of me and didn't move any more. I bent down to lift him up again and found a knife stuck in his back. That's how you found me with it in my hand."

It was a childish story that no one took seriously; and barely a week later Angelo Carboni was sentenced to the electric chair.

Detective Joseph Petrosino decided to look into the case when it seemed that everything had already been resolved. In his wanderings in disguise through the streets of the Italian section, he had in fact heard strange rumors to the effect that Angelo Carboni was going to go to the electric chair in place of someone else. But what could be the meaning of such talk? Was it possible that Carboni, who had in fact been found with the bloody weapon in his hand, could really be innocent? For several days Petrosino could not decide whether or not to launch a new investigation, which entailed the risk of being made to look foolish. But in the end, whether because the rumors of Carboni's innocence continued to be heard or because the young man was shown to be an honest working man and the father of a family, the detective made up his mind to go to work. His investigation started from scratch. He did not even want to look at the various reports on the case that had been written by the earlier investigators. Instead, he questioned the condemned man, who was in the death cell at Sing Sing awaiting execution, at great length. Carboni, however, had nothing new to add to his original story.

"I didn't kill him," he insisted. "I swear to you that he fell down while we were fighting with our fists. Maybe somebody stabbed him in the back in the dark."

Convinced of the young man's good faith, the detective looked into the victim's past. He found at once that Natale Brogno had had many enemies, among them a certain Salvatore Ceramello, a man of sixty-two who was known for his exceptional violence and who also had been in the Trinacria Café on the evening when Brogno and Carboni had quarreled.

Petrosino then went looking for Ceramello in order to question him, but he found that the man had disappeared from his home on the very night of the killing. Naturally this precipitous flight increased the detective's suspicions and he immediately launched a search for the fugitive. This became a long manhunt that lasted about a month.

While Angelo Carboni was counting the days until his execution, Joseph Petrosino was running frantically over a good part of America. He was well aware that the life of an innocent man depended on the success of his mission. Ceramello's trail took Petrosino to Jersey City, Philadelphia, Montreal and Nova Scotia, but always in vain. At the end of August, ready to admit defeat, the detective returned to New York. But it was right in New York that he once more picked up the trail of the man he was hunting. The clue came from a cousin of Ceramello whom Petrosino tracked down in the Italian section. Employing various disguises, he followed this man for days and days. He trailed him to the Bronx, then once more to Philadelphia and then to Baltimore. There the man went to an isolated house in the outskirts. It was probably the fugitive's hiding place, but Petrosino had to make certain of it before he could go into action. In order to accomplish this, he resorted to one of his customary ruses. Having made himself unrecognizable with a heavy beard, he walked confidently up to the house and knocked on the door.

"I'm from the Board of Health," he said to the woman who opened at his knock. "I was told there was a case of smallpox here." Without waiting for a reply he pushed his way into the house.

Inside he found not only the cousin whom he had been trailing for so long but also an older man absorbed in chopping wood into pieces small enough to feed the stove. Petrosino did not have a photograph of the fugitive, but he assumed all the same that his prey was within reach.

"What's your name?" he asked, pretending to be ready to write it down in his notebook.

The old man was silent a moment, as if taken by surprise. "My name is Fiani," he said finally, with a certain discomfort.

"You mean your name is Ceramello," Petrosino retorted quickly.

He took advantage of the man's bewilderment to snatch the hatchet from his hand.

The two men and the woman looked at the self-styled health agent with hatred. Meanwhile he had drawn his pistol.

"Who are you, then?" the old man asked.

"My name is Petrosino," the detective replied as he tore off his beard in a gesture full of melodrama.

A few days later Salvatore Ceramello admitted that it was he who had killed Brogno. He had followed the two men out of the Trinacria and, when they started to punch each other, he had taken advantage of the darkness to stab Brogno in the back.

Angelo Carboni was released from prison just a week before the date scheduled for his execution. Salvatore Ceramello died in the electric chair.

A few months later, on December 22, 1898, a Sicilian-born laborer, Antonio Sperduto, was wandering along the Bowery in a desperate condition. He looked extremely ill. He kept his hands clutched to his belly, and every now and then he leaned against a wall and vomited. When a policeman approached him, Sperduto tried to tell him something in his incomprehensible dialect, but it was only through gestures that he managed to convey that someone had tried to poison him. In a few hours he was with Joseph Petrosino, and finally he could explain things in his own language.

He had come to America six months before, having left his wife and their four children behind in San Piero Patti, Sicily. He had barely got off the ship in New York when a hiring agent had offered him a job digging a new subway tunnel. He had worked hard for those six months, living on virtually nothing but bread and milk. When his job had ended and he had given his foreman and the hiring agent their "cuts," he had a nest egg of one hundred and two dollars. It was just enough to bring over his family to join him.

So, the day before he was found on the Bowery, he had gone to the offices of an Italian steamship line to find out what he had to do in order to get the ticket for the voyage into his wife's hands.

When he left the offices, he saw a stranger approaching him. "He was very well dressed," Sperduto explained to Petrosino, "and he seemed glad to see me—"

"And then," the detective interrupted, "he addressed you by your name and said he had known you when you were both boys in Sicily—"

"That's right," the laborer said in astonishment. "He knew my wife's name, too."

"So you agreed to go and have a drink with him to celebrate the meeting. Right?"

"That's just what happened," Sperduto said. "But what happened after that I have no idea. All I know is that I woke up in a dark alley. I was lying in a pool of vomit and I didn't have my wallet."

Joseph Petrosino was used to such stories. For some time he had been hunting down the so-called poison gang. Its business was to learn, through various stratagems, the names and places of origin of its chosen victims. (Sperduto, for example, had supplied all the necessary information about himself and his wife to the ship line.) Thereupon a member of the gang would approach the target, pretending that they had known each other in the old country, and invite him to have a drink. The drink would be doctored with enough knockout drops to take care of a horse.

In contrast to the other victims, who always refused to cooperate with the police, Antonio Sperduto did not have to be coaxed to provide all the evidence at his disposal. And his cooperation turned out to be decisive. Within a few days Joseph Petrosino arrested the head of the gang, one Giuseppe Giuliano, as he was going home to his apartment on the fourth floor of a house on Park Street.

Giuliano tried to resist arrest, and the ensuing battle was dramatic. Their arms tight around each other, gangster and policeman rolled down the stairs together from the fourth floor to the street. But Petrosino was the stronger and he thrust Giuliano's head under a manhole cover while squeezing his throat so hard that Giuliano was almost strangled. And indeed it is quite possible that Petrosino would have finished him off if Giuliano had not had the good luck to faint.

In the following year, 1899, Joseph Petrosino rounded up the "insurance gang" as it was called; it had one hundred and twelve members. In addition to the usual frauds on insurance companies, these gentlemen had worked out a system for collecting on policies that was as ingenious as it was lethal. Pretending to be insurance salesmen, they would persuade their less sophisticated compatriots to take out life insurance on credit. The insured had his policy without having laid out a penny, for it was the friendly agent who kindly offered to advance the premium. By way of security, he asked only that the policy-holder make him the beneficiary . . . later it would be a simple matter for the buyer to change the beneficiary. It should not be necessary to add that people who bought insurance in this way seldom managed to survive longer than a year.

4. "I Warned Him"

"ANARCHIST FROM AMERICA kills King Umberto I of Italy at Monza!" the newsboys of Mulberry Street shrieked at the top of their lungs on the morning of July 30, 1900. The news made a tremendous stir in the Italian section of New York. Many people even stayed away from work and crowded into bars to hear the details recounted by those who could read the American newspapers.

In a few hours special editions were issued also by *Il Progresso italo-americano* and *l'Araldo,* two of the most widely read Italian newspapers in the United States, with long accounts of the event cabled from Italy. At the same time the Italian consul general in New York, Carlo Branchi, and the Italian ambassador in Washington, Marquis Mayor des Planches, delivered to the authorities the first notes from their government, in which it asked for the collaboration of the American police in getting to the roots of the conspiracy that had cost the life of the King of Italy.

The assassin was thirty-one-year-old Gaetano Bresci who had been born in Prato, Tuscany. He had indeed gone back to Italy from the United States; specifically, from Paterson, New Jersey, where there was a large Italian colony, almost all of whose members came from the north-central region of Italy and were connected with the anarchist movement.

The urgent requests from the Italian government, however, were not sufficient to bring about a thorough investigation. Moreover, the Americans did not evidence any great interest in the series of attacks that anarchists (almost all of them Italian) had been carrying out in Europe in recent years. Such attempts at assassination were looked on as the consequences of the absolutist—or, at any rate, inadequately democratic—systems that still persisted in the Old World. Therefore these were problems the solution of which was to be sought by the Europeans themselves; the great star-spangled Republic, serenely growing ever more prosperous under the protection of its democratic Constitution, had nothing to fear from such quarters.

As a result of this conviction, the inquiry that got under way in Paterson, in the very "den" of the anarchists, was conducted in an easygoing fashion. The local chief of police himself asserted that he had no reason for harassing citizens "who respect the American laws," as the anarchists in Paterson certainly did.

The Italian government, of course, was not pleased by this statement. In Rome, in fact, there was a general conviction that the regicide had not been the "individual act of protest" that Gaetano Bresci vainly and obstinately continued to call it, but rather the outcome of a cunning plot. It was further known that for some time Paterson had been a fortress of anarchy in which such dreaded subversives as Enrico Malatesta, Saverio Merlino, Camillo Prampolini and other exiled Italian anarchists were quite at home.

The Italian ambassador was therefore called on to address himself directly to the President of the United States and ask him, in the name of the King of Italy, to order a new investigation. William McKinley, who had been reelected only a few months earlier, decided to entrust the matter to the Secret Service. The agent who was selected to head the investigation was named Redfern. But he went back to Washington almost at once, pointing out that, because of his ignorance of the Italian language, he was absolutely incapable of executing the assignment that had been given to him.

Theodore Roosevelt, the former Police Commissioner of New York, had been elected as McKinley's Vice President. When McKinley informed him of the complication that threatened fresh problems in the country's relations with Italy, it required no great effort for Roosevelt to find a solution.

"I have just the man for this job," Roosevelt told the President. "His name is Joe Petrosino, and he's one of the best detectives in New York. He'll most certainly find a way to get himself into anarchist circles in Paterson."

A few days later, an Italian immigrant who had just come to America took a room in Bertoldi's Hotel in Paterson. He was Pietro Moretti, alias Joseph Petrosino. Bertoldi's, a small hotel of the cheapest kind, also served as a meeting place for the town's anarchists. In fact, Bresci had lived there for some time before moving in with an Irish girl, Sophie Knieland, whom he subsequently married. Petrosino, who had had the foresight to get himself a job as an unskilled laborer, stayed in the hotel for three months.

He had always felt the utmost hatred toward anarchists—not only because he was a policeman but also because he viewed as monstrous any idea of overthrowing a society such as America's, which he regarded as the finest in the world. In his view anarchists were either common criminals or dangerous maniacs to be shut up out of hand in madhouses.

With his laborer's job and his peasant's face the policeman did not arouse the slightest suspicion. In fact, he made a number of friends, pretending, though without overdoing it, to be interested in progressive and anarchist ideas. Meanwhile, he was a human sponge soaking up every detail that might prove useful to his investigation. And three months later (apparently after having used strong-arm methods with Sophie Knieland in order to extort further details on the subject of Bresci) he went back to New York with a folder filled with notes. He informed his superiors that he had come into possession of disclosures so grave that the very safety of the nation could be said to be in peril. Then he went to Washington to report in person to President McKinley and Vice President Roosevelt.

The assassination of Umberto I—according to what Petrosino said—was the result of a conspiracy set in motion in Paterson by a group of persons affiliated with the *real* Black Hand: the anarchist one. Gaetano Bresci had been chosen by lot as the executioner, having drawn the fatal number from a drum; this system was widely used in the New York underworld as well. But the most sensational discovery, according to Petrosino, was information he had unearthed to the effect that the anarchists were planning to assassinate the President of the United States himself.

The policeman's revelation was not taken very seriously. In fact McKinley received it with a patronizing smile, convinced as he was that he was the best-loved man in America. And Teddy Roosevelt, with his usual snobbish cynicism, offered no more than a witticism: "I certainly hope it will not be the anarchists who will make me President."

And that was the end of it.

According to a very widespread American superstition, Presidents elected in years that end in zero are destined to die before they complete their terms. This superstition was founded on a disturbingly repeated coincidence. President William Henry Harrison, elected in 1840, died barely a year later. Abraham Lincoln, elected in 1860, was assassinated in 1865.* James Garfield, elected in 1880, was killed the following year. And so every twenty years (for the fatal zero-year of election does indeed recur at that interval) the pattern has in fact continued, through Franklin Delano Roose-

---

*In his second term.—Translator.

velt, elected in 1940, who died in 1945,* and John F. Kennedy, elected in 1960 and assassinated in 1963.

Reelected to the Presidency in 1900, McKinley paid no attention to the legend, nor was he moved by Petrosino's warning. He was a good-natured provincial American, convinced that all that was needed to win friends was to go about patting people on the back.

"I don't have any enemies," he used to say. "Why should I be afraid?" And he firmly refused all efforts to assure his personal security. "My fellow citizens would think that I don't trust them," he would add.

That was how it was on the morning of December 6, 1901. William McKinley had gone to Buffalo to open the Pan-American Exposition, one of those huge displays that celebrate the advances of science and the conquests of man against a background of colossal machines, neoclassic statuary and patriotic bunting. That morning the President was scheduled to see "everyone who would like to meet him" in a vast pavilion that was called, in the unsophisticated rhetoric of the period, the Temple of Music.

The President's desire to shake the hand of everyone who wanted to greet him gave the Secret Service men much to think about. Jokingly, McKinley had pretended to suppose that what worried them was the fear that his hand would be seriously injured by so many pressures.

"Don't worry," he said. "My predecessor in the White House taught me a special technique for shaking hands with voters."

"It isn't only your hand that concerns us," the head of the squad replied. "Anyway, the crowd will be so big that you won't have a chance to shake hands with everybody."

"In any case they'll know I've done my best," the President insisted. "Every handshake is a guaranty of a vote."

It had proved impossible to persuade him to alter his program. His private secretary, George Cortelyou, tried to frighten him by reminding him that, according to Petrosino's report, McKinley was on the anarchists' assassination list, as were the Tsar, Emperor Wilhelm II of Germany and Emperor Franz Josef of Austria-Hungary.

*In his fourth term.—Translator.

But the President argued: "I don't fall into that category. Why should they kill me when they're perfectly free to vote against me?"

At four o'clock in the afternoon, then, William McKinley took his place on the platform set up in the center of the Temple of Music and made a sign to the ushers to show that he was ready to greet the electorate. Outside the Temple a long line of people had been waiting for hours to shake the President's hand. The police had made every effort to remove anyone who looked suspicious.

But a twenty-eight-year-old native of Poland, Leo Czolgosz, had the gift of never attracting attention. Unlike Gaetano Bresci, Czolgosz was a silent, modest fellow. He had recently lost a couple of jobs because of a series of nervous breakdowns. Finally he had gone off to the country and taken over a small farm.

In anticipation of reaching the President's platform he had wrapped a small .32-caliber Iver Johnson revolver in his handkerchief; and then he had wiped his forehead with the same handkerchief several times without anyone's noticing what was inside it.

When the line began to move, the worried Cortelyou posted himself next to the entrance. McKinley was supposed to signal to him when he was weary of shaking hands, and Cortelyou wanted to be ready to close the door.

He never got the signal. Twelve minutes after the line had begun to move, a pale young man who seemed to have one hand in a bandage stepped up to the President and shot him twice in the abdomen.

By a miracle the gunman was saved from being lynched. When the police searched him, they found in his wallet a newspaper clipping that told of Bresci's act.

In a certain sense the assassination in Buffalo represented one of the most important landmarks in Joseph Petrosino's career. Indeed, he made the most of it to gain publicity for the findings of his secret mission to Paterson.

"I warned him!" the detective told the press, making no attempt to hide his tears. "I told him the anarchist criminals wanted to kill him. But the President was too good-hearted and believed too

much in other people's goodness to take my warnings seriously."
Then he went on to explain how he had come into possession of
the secret plans that had been made prior to the murder of Mc-
Kinley.

On the question of these nonexistent plans Joseph Petrosino was
exaggerating. Indeed, it was absolutely impossible at any time to
show that Czolgosz had had contacts of any kind with anarchist
groups or movements. And the assassin himself, right up to the
moment of his execution, continued to reiterate that he had acted
on an impulse of his own. But, given the witch-hunt atmosphere
that was intensifying dangerously, it was just such statements as
those made by the Italian-American detective that "made news."

"Petrosino Warned Him"; "Italian Detective Tried to Save Mc-
Kinley"; "Anarchist Assassins' Plot Revealed by Detective Petrosino"—such were some of the headlines that the American newspapers produced. The detective's name became known throughout
the country. Some papers published—without accuracy—biographies
of him.

Furthermore, the President's death opened the doors of the White
House to Teddy Roosevelt, who otherwise, however ambitious he
was, would have had a hard time arriving at it. Thus Petrosino had
a potential protector at the summit of the nation.

The reactions of Americans generally to the anarchists were not
very different from those of the residents of New Orleans to the
Mafiosi. Here and there in the various states there were lynchings;
everywhere anyone who was identified as an anarchist was beaten
and driven out.

A. Jamowsky, a Polish anarchist who ran a little paper, very
nearly wound up on a gallows improvised in the middle of Broadway in New York. In Seattle a Jewish anarchist was bound and
immersed several times in the waters of nearby Lake Washington;
he very nearly drowned. In Paterson a laborer named Giovanni
Martini was shot with a revolver because, when he was drunk, he
had incautiously said something kind about Czolgosz. And Sophie
Knieland, who had been left in peace until now, was driven out of
Paterson by the mayor himself.

The danger that up to this time had menaced only European governments thus became an American problem as well. In order to stem the influx of criminals and subversives, the government set up a kind of concentration camp on Ellis Island, a little over a mile from the southern tip of Manhattan, to which immigrants who aroused suspicion were sent for further investigation.

Petrosino, of course, was put in charge of checking the Italians. But, as he was quickly able to see, it was much easier to spot anarchists than criminals; indeed, the criminals always came in with absolutely clean police records.

5. Under Commissioner Bingham

TOWARD THE END OF 1904 even the most skeptical had become convinced that the Black Hand was an organization with branches in every part of the country and a tie to Sicily as fundamental as that of the umbilical cord. The only opponent of this frightening theory was the Italian Ambassador in Washington, Mayor des Planches. Paradoxically, he began to grow quite angry with Petrosino. "The 'Black Hand'? Mr. Petrosino invented it to account for his own failures," the Ambassador declared.

In truth the Italian underworld had made gigantic advances in recent months. Its extortion methods in particular had been improved, and a kind of bloodless bureaucracy was supplanting sensational brutality. The "knife letters" had become as uniform as tax blanks. And while, in the past, the extortionists had been quite capable of demanding fantastic sums and then settling for fifty or a hundred dollars, now their assessments were almost always tailored to the victim's actual ability to pay.

Joseph Petrosino himself, then, had finally been brought to the point of reassessing his own convictions about the Black Hand. It was almost a ritual for him to repeat by way of justification: "It's our own stupid laws that have allowed them to organize." Nonetheless he had taken a realistic view of the new situation.

It was in this period that the detective learned of a new method of extortion that was gaining a foothold in Little Italy: the organized, universalized racket that subjected its victims to a regular tax, with fixed dates of payment, in place of the old once-and-for-all lump-sum payments. The first intimation of this new system came to him from a frightened shopkeeper in Elizabeth Street, who subsequently, however, refused to sign any statements.

"They came to see me the other evening," the man said, trembling. "There were three of them, with ugly faces, but elegantly dressed and very polite. They knew I'd received 'knife letters' in the past and so they offered me their protection. 'Just have faith in us, Don Vincenzo,' they said with their hands on their hearts, 'and from now on nobody will touch a hair of your head or your family's.' So I asked them why they were telling me this and what they wanted in return, since it seemed plain to me that they weren't the kind to be doing this out of charity. 'Just wet our whistles,' they told me."

Wetting the whistle was the name for the Sicilian system by means of which the Mafia gained domination over anyone who wanted to run any kind of business by providing him with "continuing protection"; and *whistle* became synonymous with the payments that the "beneficiary" had to make regularly to the honorable society.

Petrosino had no way of knowing it, but this system had been imported into New York City by Vito Cascio Ferro himself, the mysterious Sicilian who had vanished from sight after having been mixed up in the case of "the man in the barrel." This same Don Vito, who was held in unlimited esteem by such notable gangsters as Giuseppe Morello, Ignazio Lupo and Giuseppe Fontana, had explained to his acolytes how they must update the primitive extortion procedures then in use in New York.

"You have to skim the cream off the milk without breaking the bottle," he had elaborated in typical Mafia language. "But you're operating like two-bit punks. Try a new system. Don't throw people into bankruptcy with ridiculous demands for money. Offer them your protection instead, help them to make their businesses prosperous, and not only will they be happy to wet your whistles but they'll kiss your hands out of gratitude."

Vito Cascio Ferro's sermon did not go unheeded. In a very short time a good number of Black Hand bomb-throwers had turned into fatherly *protectors*.

Actually this racket had first appeared in Little Italy in 1903. The head of the organization was Giuseppe Morello, who deserves the highest ranking in the black book of major bosses of the Italian-American underworld. His principal collaborator was his brother-in-law, Ignazio Lupo, who performed the functions of the military commander of the gang. It was he who headed the teams instructed to punish, and sometimes to kill, those who refused to pay for protection. Others of Morello's lieutenants were Giuseppe Fontana, Carlo Costantino, Pietro Inzerillo, the Terranova brothers, Ignazio Milone and Antonino Passananti.

It should be pointed out here that the English word *racket* soon began to be part of the slang of the New York underworld. Even though its meaning was quite different, its sound resembled that of *ricatto, extortion,* to the Sicilian ear. A very great number of such semantic mutations took place in the language that the Italians in America brought into being. Not many people know, for instance, that even today, in certain circles of the Italian-American criminal world, it is customary to indicate one's approval of a given project by saying: "Goose by me." The origin of this incomprehensible phrase goes back to the earliest days of the Italian immigration, when the American expression, *okay,* which was universally used, was changed by the immigrants into *oca,* an Italian word that they then retranslated into its English equivalent, *goose.*

In the early part of 1905 the sudden resurgence of Italian criminality in new forms persuaded the Board of Aldermen of New York to end its opposition to the creation of a squad of exclusively Italian policemen.

"They've finally granted your request," McAdoo told Petrosino. "You are now authorized to set up an Italian squad. You yourself will select its members."

"How many will there be?" Petrosino asked anxiously.

"Not more than five." The Commissioner's reply was a blow.

"Five men aren't very many to keep a section with five hundred thousand people in line," Petrosino observed with a certain tartness. But he did not protest; he was used to having things squeezed out drop by drop.

"For the present you'll have to handle it yourself," McAdoo concluded ambiguously.

Thus the Italian Branch was officially founded on January 20, 1905 in Detective Petrosino's two-room apartment. Its members consisted of his devoted associate, Maurise Bonoil, born of French and Irish parentage on the Lower East Side, who spoke Sicilian better than he did English; Peter Dondero, George Silva, John Lagomarsini and Ugo Cassìdi, who preferred to be called Hugh Cassidy, like the then famous gunman, Butch Cassidy.

With the help of these men Petrosino set up a real intelligence center with dozens of informers posted in strategic places throughout Little Italy. Meetings were held periodically, first in Petrosino's own apartment and later in an old house on Waverly Place in Greenwich Village. On their own, working virtually without a break, Petrosino and his men put together the first list of Italian criminals operating in the entire state of New York, with well-filled folders available for use whenever the American government might make up its mind to send these undesirable residents back where they came from.

In addition, the Italian Branch began piling up arrests and accusations, and Petrosino initiated his associates into his own methods. "If the courts send these criminals back into the streets," he said, "we'll make life so tough for them that they'll have to clear out whatever way they can."

This propensity for using his hands occasionally got the detective into serious trouble. On one occasion, for example, his conduct was openly censured by the Board of Aldermen as a result of protests by a member from Brooklyn, who accused the policeman of having "knocked out more teeth than a professional dentist."

Petrosino himself and his colleagues were arrested on another occasion, but for very different reasons. This curious episode took place in May of 1905.

For several days the Irish policeman on the beat in the Waverly Place area noticed a great coming and going of suspicious individuals who hung round a house that faced Washington Square. He questioned the janitor's wife, but all that she could tell him was that an Italian had rented an apartment on the fourth floor and was often visited by very dubious types. "If you ask me," the woman said, "they're in the 'Black Hand.' "

The policeman was convinced of this too and he hurried off to the captain of the Third District, which covered the neighborhood. A few hours later several dozen policemen surrounded the house while the captain himself led others, guns in hand, in a forced entry into the apartment under suspicion. The dozen or so men in the room looked at them in utter bewilderment. At an authoritative gesture from the thickset man who seemed to be their leader, however, all of them kept silent and did not offer any resistance.

Securely handcuffed, the suspects were taken away in the patrol wagon that was waiting at the door. A large crowd that had gathered applauded the police enthusiastically.

During the ride the thickset man turned to the police captain. "You've made a big mistake, captain," the detective said. "My name is Petrosino, and these three are my men. The rest are our informers."

For a moment or two, while his face grew purple, the captain said nothing. "Then why didn't you tell me right away?" he asked at last. "Now it's too late. Too many people saw us take you away, and now we'd all look like fools. Think how the reporters would laugh if they ever found out about it—to say nothing of the gangsters."

Three months after this misadventure, the Italian Branch scored its first sensational success with the case of the mushroom picker.

Van Cortlandt Park in the Bronx, at the northern tip of New York City, is still a great expanse of green today. At the beginning of the century it was thickly wooded. It was there that the body of a young man with thirty-six stab wounds was found on August 13, 1905, a Sunday.

The discovery was made by a forty-year-old textile worker, Frank Lo Cascio, who had gone deep into the woods in his hunt for mushrooms. Terrified by the sight of the body, Lo Cascio ran to the nearest police station to report the incident. The poor fellow could never have imagined what serious trouble would be made for him by his conscientious act.

During his mushroom hunt that morning he had encountered two other Italians in the park. They told him that they had lost their way, and they asked him to give them directions to Yonkers, an industrial town just above New York City. Lo Cascio had a few words with the two strangers, chiefly with the younger one, who seemed very elated.

"You know," he said, "this is a very big day for me. In a few hours I'll see my brother again after years of looking for him."

The other man asked whether there was a good restaurant in the neighborhood, and Lo Cascio told them how to get to a place called The Promised Land. "You'll see it as soon as you get out of the woods," he added.

Before they left, the younger man offered Lo Cascio a Cremona cigar. "Smoke it to my health," he said as he started off, "because today I'm happy."

A few hours after this encounter Frank Lo Cascio discovered the body. The victim was the young man who had offered him the cigar.

This strange story did not hold water for the suspicious police-men in the Bronx. Frank Lo Cascio wound up in jail. Luckily for him, the case was turned over to Joseph Petrosino because the victim was Italian.

The detective sergeant began his investigation with his customary aggressive approach. After he had listened to the policemen who had made the arrest, he sent for Lo Cascio. The mushroom picker came into the room white and trembling.

"Get undressed," Petrosino ordered.

"Here? In front of everybody?" the poor man asked, shaking harder. For days he had been living in a nightmare.

"Take off your clothes, your shoes, everything," Petrosino said.

The man obeyed without further protest. When he was com-pletely naked, he was ordered to turn slowly in a full circle as the detective snapped out commands in an impersonal voice.

"Please note," Petrosino then said to the other policemen, "that there isn't even a scratch on any part of this man's body." A general murmur of agreement followed. "All right," Petrosino continued. "We know that the victim's body had thirty-six stab wounds, plus scratches and bruises. Therefore it's obvious that he defended him-self vigorously. Presumably he did some injury to his attacker. So to me it seems quite clear: this man is innocent."

Only then did Frank Lo Cascio realize that Petrosino was getting him out of his troubles, and, naked as he was, he threw himself on the floor to kiss the detective's feet. Petrosino brushed him aside with a gesture of irritation. "Just be prepared to testify when the time comes," he said. But, when the time did come, Lo Cascio took good care not to appear; the first experience had been enough for him.

Meanwhile a policeman named Alex De Martino, who was later to join the Italian Branch, had made an important discovery. In the victim's blood-soaked pockets he had found a paper bearing a name and ardress: Sabbato Gizzi, P.O. Box 239, Lambertville, New Jersey. The men of the Italian Branch had also done a good job. Peter Dondero dug up a subway conductor who remembered having noticed two men get off the train at Van Cortlandt Park, which was the last stop. Hugh Cassidy found a passenger on the same train whom the two strangers had asked for directions to Yonkers. One of them had offered him an Italian cigar, a Cremona, the band of which he had kept.

At that time a large number of Italians were employed in the construction of a railway in Lambertville. Almost all of them were Sicilian laborers. Sabbato Gizzi was one of them. He evidenced a certain surprise when two policemen arrived to take him to New York, but he did not seem particularly worried about it.

Later Petrosino led him into the morgue and uncovered the victim's corpse. "Do you know this man?" he asked.

Gizzi looked at the lacerated body. "I know him," he replied. "He's my friend Antonio Torsiello; he was working with me on the railroad until a few days ago. Then he left."

The story that Gizzi told Petrosino corroborated what the mushroom picker had said. Antonio Torsiello, who was twenty-one, had come to America two years before in search of his elder brother, Vito, from whom the family had heard nothing for a long time.

"Antonio couldn't read and write," Gizzi said, "but he wasn't stupid. He began his search with plenty of thought. He even went to the point of putting advertisements in all the Italian papers in the country. A few weeks ago, finally, he got the letter he'd been waiting for so long. It was from his brother, Vito. Vito wrote that he'd become a rich businessman in Yonkers and he invited Antonio to come and live with him."

"When exactly did Antonio leave Lambertville?" Petrosino asked.

"I'm not quite sure. Maybe at the end of the month. I remember that he waited for his pay, took all his savings and sold the few things he had. If I'm not mistaken, he'd managed to get together at least five hundred dollars."

Men from the Italian Branch were sent to Yonkers to find whether in fact there was a businessman there named Torsiello. The result of the investigation, as Petrosino expected, was negative. "It seemed unthinkable to me," he said, "that this Vito could have lured his brother into such a trap."

In the next few days, while the newspapers were asserting that the murder seemed fated to remain unsolved, Petrosino made up his mind to go to Lambertville himself and question Sabbato Gizzi again.

"There's one thing you could explain to me," the detective said to the laborer. "If Torsiello couldn't read or write, who wrote the advertisements for him? You, maybe?"

"No, sir!" Gizzi seemed almost angry. "I can't read or write either. For things like that we depend on a very educated man from our village. His name is Antonio Strollo and he works with us on the railroad."

"Where can I find this Strollo?"

"At the bicycle races, without a doubt," Gizzi said. "On holidays he always takes part in the bicycle races. He's our champion."

Petrosino spoke to Strollo at the end of a race in which the cyclist had placed third. He had no hesitation about admitting that he was the man who had been with Torsiello in Van Cortlandt Park. By way of explaining his not having come forward, he said: "You know, after I read what had happened to that poor mushroom picker, I decided not to go to the police. With us Italians they're always so suspicious."

"You're right, Mr. Strollo," Petrosino agreed, with that matter-of-fact manner that he was so good at assuming when he wanted to inspire confidence. "Now, though, you ought to just tell me how things happened. You understand. . ."

So, feeling quite safe, Strollo gave the detective his version of their affair. He admitted that it was he who had written the advertisements for Torsiello and read him the letter that he had received from his brother, Vito.

"Torsiello was very glad to have found him again," Strollo went on. "He even asked me to go to Yonkers with him, and I agreed . . . Poor kid, he was so ignorant that he certainly would have gotten lost. Well, at a certain point we were walking through Van Cortlandt Park and we ran into a well-dressed man whom Antonio immediately recognized as his brother. I left them there while they were still hugging each other."

This conversation was held in the locker-room, where Strollo had gone to change clothes after the race. The detective was eying him closely, and suddenly Petrosino noticed that there was a big bandage on Strollo's right leg.

"What happened to you?" Petrosino asked, sounding concerned. "I'll bet you haven't even had it disinfected. Let me see, let me see —I know something about these things."

Strollo was unable to resist the policeman's friendly persistence. "I cut myself at home with a pair of scissors," he explained, as Petrosino was taking the bandage off his leg.

"That's a very deep cut," Petrosino commented. "It looks like a knife wound."

Petrosino managed to get the young cyclist to go back to New York with him that same evening. If Strollo had refused, the detective would have had no ground for requesting his extradition from New Jersey. But Strollo was so sure of himself, so sure that he was making an ass out of this stupid policeman, that he immediately assented to Petrosino's request for his cooperation.

In New York Joseph Petrosino changed his tone. Standing with his face to a wall, Antonio Strollo was thoroughly searched and in his pocket the police found a letter from Antonio Torsiello to Vito, his brother, saying that he was about to go to Yonkers.

"Why didn't you mail this?" Petrosino demanded.

"Because it's a rough draft of the one that Antonio actually did send to his brother. Can't you see how carelessly it's written? I really don't know why I kept it in my pocket," Strollo said confidently. And nothing could make him contradict himself.

Strollo having been remanded to custody as a material witness, Petrosino set off again for Lambertville, where he now had the leisure to search the room in which Antonio Torsiello had lived. He did not, in fact, find very much: only the torn envelope that had contained his brother's letter. The envelope was crumpled, but he could still read the postmark beside the two-cent stamp: "Lambertville, N.J. July 26, 1905."

"Do you recognize this envelope?" Petrosino asked Strollo when he had returned to New York.

"Sure. It's from the letter from Vito inviting Antonio to stay with him in Yonkers."

"Who read that letter to Antonio Torsiello?"

"I did, of course! You know very well that he couldn't read."

"Of course I know it. And that's why you figured you didn't have to go to Yonkers to mail it." The detective's voice went suddenly hard. "Naturally; that poor guy would never have been able to make out the postmark. But I can read, unluckily for you."

Not even this proof that the letter had been mailed from Lambertville and not from Yonkers could make Strollo confess. He continued to insist on his innocence, hinting that probably some other acquaintance of the victim had laid the ambush for him.

At this stage Petrosino did not push interrogation too far. The man was obviously a tough specimen. Even under torture he would not have confessed. Furthermore, the evidence thus far in hand was totally inadequate to bring him to trial.

As patient as he was stubborn, the detective went back once more to Lambertville. He went to the post office and asked the four persons who worked there whether by any chance one or another of them recognized the envelope. He was lucky; Miss Elaine McNeil identified it at once.

"I remember it very well," she explained, "for two reasons. One is that I was surprised when I saw that it was to someone in town. Lambertville is so little, you know. . . . The other reason is that I was also surprised when the customer asked me for a two-cent stamp. 'For letters inside New Jersey you only need a one-cent stamp,' I told him. But he insisted on a two, as if the letter were going to another state."

Miss McNeil's description of the customer was an exact match to Strollo's.

But even with this further evidence in hand Joseph Petrosino did not feel too safe. He knew the distrust of courts for circumstantial evidence; he knew how they tended to set anyone free as soon as the slightest shadow of doubt appeared. So, after he had conferred with his colleagues, he decided to plant a stool pigeon in Strollo's cell. This informer, whose name was G. B. Repetto, spent two weeks in the cell and succeeded in gaining Strollo's confidence. Some time later, in fact, Repetto received a letter from Strollo asking him to appear as a witness at the trial. Repetto was supposed to testify that he had seen Strollo, the day before the murder, wearing a grey suit and rust-colored shoes. But these were the clothes that the murderer had acquired after the crime in order to get rid of the blood-stained things he was wearing.

Repetto (who was also to become a policeman in the Italian Branch) did indeed appear in court, but not to say what the killer expected. Antonio Strollo was sentenced to the electric chair. He was executed on March 11, 1908.

A year after its establishment, the New York City Police Department's Italian Branch found a powerful protector in the person of Theodore Bingham, who had become Police Commissioner as of January 1, 1906. "General" Bingham, as he liked people to call him even though, in actuality, he had never gotten beyond a colonelcy in the army, was very authoritarian, very able and very ambitious. A personal friend of President Teddy Roosevelt, close to the most influential circles of the Republican Party, and very well regarded in the financial community, he was aiming very high. And the post of Police Commissioner, as he very well knew, could serve as a first-class springboard.

"From this moment on," he stated when he was appointed, "the goal of my life shall be to crush the 'Black Hand' and to destroy these vile foreign criminals who have come to disrupt the serenity of our peaceful land."

In these circumstances it was natural that Bingham should depend heavily on Joseph Petrosino and, at the same time, afford him all possible support. As a start, Bingham asked Petrosino for a detailed report on the activities of the Italian Branch and the facilities available to it. Petrosino, of course, did not have to be asked twice.

Having dealt with the handicaps imposed on his squad and the necessity of enlarging it, he wrote in his report:

The United States has now become the garbage dump for all the criminality and banditry in Italy, and especially in Sicily and Calabria.

A few years ago the French government decided to clean up the Italian quarter of Tunis as a result of the great number of crimes that were being committed there. In fact, Tunisia was at that time the favorite country of the Sicilian underworld. The investigations and roundups made by the French police led to the arrest and expulsion of more than ten thousand persons.

And where did all these Italian jailbirds go? They came here, naturally, and Uncle Sam took them in with open arms. They came here, and now they live and prosper on extortions, robberies, illicit operations of all kinds.

Unfortunately the police cannot do anything about them because the American laws hamstring them. Here in New York we have men like Vincenzo Vantone, who was expelled from Tunisia because he was suspected of twenty killings, and we can do absolutely nothing about him because his papers are in order.

One of the proposals that I have backed for years and for the realization of which, General, I rely on your cooperation, is the enactment of a law that will make it possible to arrest or to expel as undesirable aliens those persons who are shown to be wanted or to have been in jail in their countries of origin. I suppose, for example, that it would be easy enough to persuade the Italian government to send us the record of every criminal who has moved to America.

As far as the honest part of the Italian population is concerned, an educational campaign ought to be launched to make them understand that the laws are the same for everybody. The inhabitants of my native country, in fact, do not have constitutional rights like ours and they are always afraid of the established authorities. As a result, one of the first obstacles that my men and I run up against is the difficulty of getting one Italian to testify against another. In many cases, when we have already established the identity of an extortionist, we are compelled to drop the matter because the victim refuses to help us.

Another thing that should be done is to make a law forbidding several families to live in the same apartment. This, incidentally, would break up the gangs.

Also pushcarts ought to be prohibited, because they are used to transport bombs to be thrown at businesses or houses that are targets. It would also be necessary to prohibit or restrict the sale of explosives among Italians; licenses should be issued only to those who could prove their honesty and integrity.

But the most important thing would be to make our Penal Laws more severe, "more Italian." The trouble with the immigrants who come from Italy, and in particular from Sicily and Calabria, is that they do not know how to make the proper use of the freedom that they find here. In the country from which they come, the Penal Code is designed specifically to deal with their ignorance and their hotheadedness. There they feel the hand of the law always pressing on their shoulders. Because there the Code is designed for the protection of society. So, when they arrive here and find that our Code, on the contrary, is designed to protect the citizen, they feel free to let loose all their lowest instincts.

We have no way of knowing whether, as he wrote his report, Petrosino was hoping to get concrete results from Bingham after he had spent so many years reiterating the same ideas to McAdoo. But, as we have said, Bingham was a different type. He at once devoted himself to the concerns of the Italian Branch and initiated plans for its enlargement; but he won the gratitude of the Italian policemen above all because he frequently took their side in political disputes. When, for example, some member of the Board of Aldermen protested for the nth time against the excessively brutal methods adopted by Petrosino, Bingham leaped to his feet indignantly.

"I am the Police Commissioner," he shouted. "I am responsible for everything that my men do. Consequently any accusation directed against a member of my department is an accusation directed against me personally." Then, as he calmed down, he added: "Petrosino is one of our best detectives. With a handful of men he has to keep thousands of Italian criminals in line. Of course he has to use his hands now and then, but we ought to let him alone. He knows the Italians better than we do."

"At last," Petrosino said the next day when he read the account of the session in *The New York Times,* "we've found a commissioner who understands us." Yes, Theodore Bingham grasped the importance of a loyal, efficient Italian squad to be used for destroying, as he put it, "the gangs of Italian criminals and their anarchist accomplices."

Within four months the Italian Branch had grown to twenty-five men, plus a detachment of ten more men in Brooklyn under the command of Sergeant Antonio Vachris. The results were immediately notable: hundreds of Italian criminals were arrested and many crimes were disclosed as a result of testimony from citizens who now felt that they enjoyed greater protection. At the same time the press also published some statistics. It was stated, for instance, that the Italian squad's work had reduced the ranks of the Black Hand by fifty per cent. This figure was simply snatched out of thin air, but there was no doubt that something had in fact been accomplished.

In November of 1906 the Italian Branch became the Italian Legion. Petrosino was promoted to a lieutenancy. The first Italian who had succeeded in becoming an officer in an American police force celebrated the occasion with a few friends (Bonoil, Vachris, Dondero and De Martino) in Vincent Saulino's restaurant, at the corner of Lafayette and Spring Streets.

Vincent Saulino came from Agnoni, in the Province of Campobasso, but he had lived in Manhattan for thirty-five years. His wife, Maria, was an excellent cook and her culinary achievements had brought renown to the place. Petrosino was a steady customer of theirs. He used to telephone from his office to announce his arrival, and he would find his table ready. Waiting made him extremely nervous. He would eat rapidly and go right back to work. Only recently had be begun to linger in the restaurant to chat briefly with Adelina, the owner's daughter, who had come back to live with them after the death of her husband, Edward Vinti. The Vintis had had no children.

The solid policeman's attentions to the widow had not escaped old Vincent. He had discussed the matter with his wife, in fact, and voiced a certain perplexity. Unquestionably a widowed daughter represented a major problem; nevertheless, to let her marry a policeman . . . ? Was there not, among other things, the risk of her being widowed again? But Maria Saulino was less of a pessimist and, besides, she liked this closemouthed customer of hers. At that time Joseph Petrosino was forty-six and Adelina Vinti was thirty-seven.

On the evening of the celebration of his promotion to the

lieutenancy, Petrosino stayed longer than usual in the Lafayette Street restaurant. A few bottles of Chianti were emptied, and the wine gave him courage to make his proposal to Adelina.

"You too must be very lonely," he said to her. "We could get along well together."

Adelina nodded assent. She knew that sooner or later Petrosino was going to propose to her; and, as she is supposed to have said later, she did not expect him to do it in substantially different terms.

Adelina and Giuseppe were married on the first Sunday of April, 1907, in the old St. Patrick's Church in Mott Street. The ceremony was performed by Msgr. Patrick J. La Valle, an old friend of the bridegroom. The Italian Legion attended in full strength, and among the guests of honor was Theodore Bingham. After the wedding luncheon, which was given in the Saulinos' restaurant, the couple went to their new home on the fourth floor of 233 Lafayette Street, a four-room apartment that Petrosino had rented from one J. A. March.

At their age they dispensed with a honeymoon. Petrosino was too involved in his work and, for her part, Adelina made no demands. She was a sensible woman who was fully aware what kind of life lay ahead of her if she married the most famous but also the most hated policeman in New York. Indeed, she became accustomed to spending almost all her time in the house. She learned not to become upset over the threats in the anonymous letters that arrived periodically, and not even to show herself at a window, especially at night, lest she provide a target for some unknown sniper. It was not a fine life, but the Petrosinos were happy in their fashion.

Joseph Petrosino was overloaded with work because a new immigration law had just been passed that made it possible to expel undesirables from the country. The lieutenant and his men were therefore extremely busy collecting information and material for their files on the Italian underworld.

The law that had been so long awaited became effective in July of 1907. It had been substantially weakened, however, by a series of limiting amendments, and in the end it still left a number of loopholes for the criminals. Under this law, in fact, a criminal could be deported from the United States only if he were identified as such prior to his third year of residence in the country. In practice the law was ineffectual for the most noted gangsters, such as Morello, Lupo & Co., since they had been residents of the United States for more than three years. The law also established, however, that the residential limitation did not apply to the expulsion or extradition from America of those criminals who were still being pursued by the police of their own countries.

Petrosino pored over the new legislation for hours before he went to see General Bingham. "This law wouldn't get a spider out of its web," he said. "Almost every criminal that we've managed to get into our files has been in America more than three years. As for the new ones, it will take us three years to find out who they are unless the Italian government helps us."

"The Italian government won't help us," Bingham replied. "This we can be sure of. So we'll have to go it alone."

"How?" the policeman asked.

"I'll explain at the proper time, lieutenant. You and I together, you'll see, will finally smash this gang of criminals and anarchists that your native land has given us."

The first victim of the new immigration law was Enrico Alfano, known as Erricone (Big Henry), the notorious head of the Neapolitan Camorra, who was being vigorously hunted at that time because he was accused of having killed a couple named Cuocolo in Naples.

Erricone had fled to America and had at once taken out his first papers for naturalization. Petrosino made the arrest himself in theatrical fashion. Having found out where Alfano was hiding, in a disreputable cheap dive on the Lower East Side, the detective went there alone after a dramatic telephone call to the top crime reporter of *The New York Times* (who rewarded him, of course, with a highly flattering account of the capture).

Erricone was sitting at a table with six other types who looked anything but respectable. As Petrosino entered he said from the doorway, characteristically: "My name is Petrosino." There was a moment of silence; everyone looked at the short, stocky man in the derby hat who had not moved from the doorway.

"Enrico Alfano," he said, "your're under arrest. Come with me."

Taken by surprise, Erricone got up, looked at his men, who had not budged, and, assuming that there must be a whole regiment of policemen waiting outside, silently held out his wrists for the handcuffs.

Throwing Enrico Alfano out of the United States, however, was not an easy job. The lawyers that his friends retained to defend him managed to erect innumerable obstacles. They came very close to winning the case. In the end, since Alfano had sailed for New York from Le Havre, they prevailed on the court to order him deported not to Italy but to France. For once, however, the Italian police were ready to cooperate, and, as a result of a speedy agreement with the French, the notorious Big Henry found a squadron of police waiting at Le Havre to escort him directly to the Italian border.

6. A Speech by the Honorable Giuseppe De Felice Giuffrida

THOSE AMERICANS WHO, LIKE PETROSINO, still relied on Italian cooperation to dam the tide of criminals were grossly deceiving themselves. The government in Rome did not have even the slightest intention of interfering in any way with the chaotic torrent of emigrants, which represented a dual and eminently convenient safety valve for the ruling class of the time.

"Emigration," *Il Corriere della Sera** declared, timidly attempting to sound an alarm, "which is widely regarded as an economic safety valve for so many of the poor and heavily populated towns of southern Italy, is regarded by others as a moral safety valve for the spontaneous elimination of the more dangerous elements of the local criminal world that comes with it. But to have encouraged

*A Milanese newspaper; then, as now, one of the most important in Italy.—Translator.

74

the departure of legions of offenders and frequently to close our eyes to that exodus entails a much greater harm to us."

Such warnings were to all intents and purposes a waste of time. The immediate advantages of the "safety valve" were too over-whelming, in comparison with the disadvantages, to permit any serious consideration of giving them up. In addition to the factors of "economic safety" and "moral clean-up" noted by *Il Corriere della Sera,* moreover, there were even more cogent reasons for assisting the mass departure of the undesirables. Chief among them was the relationship between the Mafia and politics: the Mafia helped the politicians win elections, so the politicians had to help the Mafia when things got bad.

It is a matter of common knowledge that, when they reached Palermo, the Piedmontese* discovered that the Mafia already existed and, indeed, they used it at first for their own purposes. Only later, about 1877, did the old Piedmontese police officials sent into Sicily organize a really energetic cleanup of the area. Naturally, they did not *tear up the roots* of the organization, but the fact remains that for more than a dozen years the Mafia seemed to have vanished. Undeniably, however, it reappeared when Giovanni Giolitti** became a leading figure in national politics. Giolitti did not know the south (he never went farther south than Rome) and, from all the available evidence, he looked on it only as a useful source of votes. In fact, in order to assure the election of deputies whom he could trust (the famous *ascari****), he simply closed his eyes to incidents that, had they happened north of Rome, would have roused him to the most vocal indignation.

"With Giolitti's accession to power," Renato Candida wrote in his *Storia della Mafia (History of the Mafia),* "the real golden age

---

*That is, the forces that brought about the unification of Italy.—Translator

**A Piedmontese politician of both Left and Right, as well as, occasionally, Center, who launched Italy's war on Tripoli and who later tacitly approved Mussolini's violence against the Socialists and materially furthered his rise to power.—Translator.

***Originally, native troops from Italy's African possessions; the term was applied in derogation to these southern Italian members of Parliament.—Translator.

of the Mafia began. In order to be certain of favorable electoral
results, Giolitti, who knew very little of the character of the Mafia,
preferred to regard its branches from the point of view of the
number of votes that they could rally to the government party.
Politicians, officials and policemen overwhelmed the Mafia leaders
with favors. And everyone knows how the elections came out in
those days."

In their turn, the Mafiosi immediately recognized the magnitude
of the opportunities offered them by the electoral system, and at
once they transformed themselves into vote-getters. Thus the
boldest, the most violent, and the shrewdest wound up by combin-
ing the functions of the Mafia *capo* (chief) with those of the ward
boss in their respective districts.

In the turn-of-the-century years the Mafia, which had been
predominantly a provincial and agricultural phenomenon, was
transplanted to the heart of the cities. Extortion and *protection* became sources of income as lucrative as the traditional cattle rustling.
Corruption or threats of force helped Mafia men to infiltrate the
banks, the public bodies and the government departments. The
cancer multiplied swiftly throughout western Sicily. As if this were
not enough, these same years saw the birth of the so-called *Mafia
di ritorno,* the homecoming Mafia, composed of men who in their
day had fled to America and who were now able to return (thanks
to some friend in Parliament) and take up where they had left off,
their skill and cruelty sharpened by their experience on the other
side of the ocean. Those were black years for Sicily, much blacker
than those of our own time, grave though the present may be. A
large part of the island was in the hands of "big shots" and Mafiosi
deputies.

In order to present a detailed picture of the situation as it was
seen from the Left, I introduce here the official transcript of a
speech that Giuseppe De Felice Giuffrida,* a Socialist deputy from

---

*Giuseppe De Felice Giuffrida (1869–1920) was an ardent Socialist. A
leading spokesman for the Fasci Siciliani in 1893–94 [the political group
formed by the exploited Sicilian miners in 1890; it had nothing at all to do
with Mussolini's Fasci, which simply appropriated the term—Translator], he

Catania, delivered in the Chamber of Deputies on November 23, 1899.

The President of the Chamber: The Honorable De Felice Giuffrida has the floor.

DE FELICE GIUFFRIDA: It is not my place to continue the discussion from the point at which it was left by my friend Bissolati.* He spoke of a government that reduces or denies the freedom that, in contrast, it permits to criminal associations.

So I will redeem the honor of southern Italy that the Honorable Di Martino, Mayor of Palermo, says has been stained by some and that the Honorable Casale believes has been compromised by others.

Southern Italy, and Sicily in particular, are *not* areas dedicated to the growth of crime; they are, rather, victims of a political and economic organization that compels the commission of criminal acts desired, protected, or indeed engendered by the government.

VARIOUS MEMBERS: Hear, hear! . . . That's the truth!

DE FELICE GIUFFRIDA: Since there has already been mention of the Camorra, of hooligans, and of other associations with criminal purposes, I, who am talking about the Mafia, with which all Italy is concerned at this time, ought to make an essential distinction. And this distinction is that, while the other associations for criminal purposes are formed only from the lowest depths of society, the sick part of the community, the Mafia, on the other hand, has various levels that shape it and sustain it. The lowest stratum, which is the best, is what is recruited in the working classes, which fear and more or less tolerate the influence of the Mafia. Above this there is a very dreaded stratum: the police. Then comes the highest level: the arrogant burgher, the gentleman, the Mafioso in kid gloves.

In this distinction I perceive the reason why in other parts of

---

was arrested and sentenced to twenty-two years in prison after the state of siege was lifted [in 1894, when the Fasci had enrolled workers in many more areas than only the sulphur mines, Premier Francesco Crispi proclaimed a state of siege for the whole of Sicily—Translator]. He was freed by amnesty in 1896, after Crispi's government had fallen. While he was in prison he had been elected a deputy both from Rome and from Catania, but the Parliamentary leadership would not ratify his election. He was a friend and follower of Filippo Turati [a major Italian Socialist—Translator].—Author.

*Leonida Bissolati-Bergamaschi, a prominent Socialist who died in 1920.—Translator.

Italy it has been possible to crush some of these criminal associations that have appeared there and why it has not been possible to overcome the Mafia in Sicily. It has not been possible because in Sicily the only aim, in all periods, of all governments, has been to strike at the weakest and least responsible part. Contrariwise, those who support it and make use of it have been left in peace, secure, powerful: undisturbed the public-safety forces, undisturbed the arrogant middle class in whose homes the Mafia meets.

You have begun by proposing, in less than six months, some ten thousand *ammonizioni** in the province of Palermo alone. You have tried new methods, restrictive laws, violence; you have had special legislation from the Chamber; you have abused all the laws, including the previous summary laws, but the result has always been the same: negative.

Do you see? The Notarbartolo trial teaches the lesson!

Look at the peasant, the peasant in the two or three provinces plagued by the Mafia. He does not have truly criminal tendencies, but he is dominated by the Mafia because he is not protected by the laws.

Hence it becomes obligatory for this unfortunate wretch, especially if he is marooned in the center of the island, to bow his head and submit to the abuses of the new boss. On the other hand, the day he can show signs of a certain criminal potential, the day he can commit a couple of crimes, go peacefully to jail if he is arrested, come out again unpunished through the protection of the Mafia boss or the no-less-Mafioso deputy, that day, I said, he becomes a power (voices from the Left: "Excellent! . . . Hear, hear!"), he is much more respected and he is hired to perform better-paid jobs. Immediately the poor share-cropper becomes a working-man with a steady wage, follows the boss on his business trips . . . protects the deputy in his elections . . .

Is it not this climate in which you compel him to live that has made a criminal out of an honest man? No one can assert, gentlemen, that the Sicilian peasant enrolls in the Mafia because he has criminal tendencies. Quite the contrary! I've seen him very close up, this peasant, and I have esteemed him all the more when you have condemned him.

---

*An *ammonizione* was a judicial proceeding imposing specific restrictions (not always identical) on offenders and potential offenders.—Translator.

A large part of the troubles in Sicily, the war against the high-ups—that is, the upper classes—has no origin other than the arrogance against which the peasant rebels when he can.

And that the Sicilian peasant's character is good I have also observed whenever he has been in a position to feel that he is protected by a collective force that he never knew before. When the workers' Fasci came into being and unfurled their banners of social justice to the winds of freedom, the peasants saw a new strength in the Fasci; they understood it and, abandoning the criminal association that is called the Mafia, they enrolled in the workers' Fasci. And the Mafia vanished wherever it was possible to set up a section of the Fasci.

By way of further convincing the Chamber, I will recall an avowal made by the Honorable Giolitti. After an interrogation by the Honorable Paternostro on the conditions of the public-safety forces in Sicily, the Honorable Giolitti, who was then Premier, acknowledged that the number of crimes reported during the period when the workers' Fasci were functioning had diminished in comparison with the past, while the number of crimes that were solved had risen.

What all this means is that the day when the Sicilian worker sees that he is protected against the violence of those who exploit him, that day he gives free rein to his honest nature. And how could things be otherwise? Now, if someone inflicts violence on a peasant, to whom can the victim turn? I put the question to the Honorable Pelloux.*

Perhaps to the public authorities? Hah! the authorities who are responsible for public safety regard the peasant as an enemy; they are designed, are established, function almost for the service of his master.

Can he turn to the Ministry of Justice? Summonses are not issued except when requested by the masters.

So he has to be satisfied to get word of this violence to someone in the Mafia, and at once the Mafia sees to it that he gets that proper reparation that he would not have been able to obtain through either the police or the courts.

I should like to ask the Sicilians who are members of this Cham-

---

*Premier Luigi Pelloux, a reactionary who sponsored much repressive and antidemocratic legislation.—Translator.

ber, particularly those from the provinces of Palermo and Girgenti: when you or your families have suffered losses as a result of thefts committed in Sicily, do you turn, have you ever turned to the public authorities? And, in the event that you have occasionally gone to the police, have you ever had the good fortune to see the thief tracked down and the stolen goods recovered?

Ah! No one answers because everyone knows that, if he wants to get something back, no other means in Sicily exists—because the police force is incompetent, because the courts do not function—than that of turning to the Mafia. That is why this institution is not the shame of the island but (turning toward the government bench) it is the shame of you who keep it alive. (Applause from the Left.)

The second level in the structure of the criminal association is the police. Of the police the Honorable Bonfandini, who was not under suspicion rather, as my friend Pansini suggests, suspicion might have been directed against him in the opposite sense, wrote this: "The official Mafia existed under the Bourbons and the Italian government has done nothing to destroy it; on the contrary, the official Mafia has made the police extremely loathsome to the honest population, which sees the police force as an association of malefactors protected by the government."

Nor let it be said that this opinion is obsolete. I will cite another, more recent view.

Subsequent to a theft of six hundred thousand lire from the Deposit and Discount Bank of Catania, the perpetrator of which was not arrested though his identity was known to everyone, the mayor of the city himself, accompanied by a former deputy, went to the Public Prosecutor to protest. This official, who had just arrived, replied: "I know his name too, but what can I do if I find all the authorities in a conspiracy against justice? Do you want me to go ahead? Very well, I will do so, but I will have to have this individual arrested before I issue the warrant for his arrest, because, if I issued the warrant and turned it over to the public authorities for execution, they would get him out of town." (Murmurs in the Chamber.)

This is historical fact. If you wish, I am prepared to give the names.

HONORABLE PONTANO: No, no.

DE FELICE GIUFFRIDA: In fact, when there is a robbery in Sicily, or, rather, when major crimes are committed, don't ask who planned them: it is always the public-safety forces! (Laughter.)

HONORABLE GATTORNO, A PIEDMONTESE DEPUTY: But these are things from another world! (Loud laughter.)

DE FELICE GIUFFRIDA: Some time ago there was a murder in Catania. A man went into a gun shop, bought a pistol, killed another man and gave himself up to the Royal Carabinieri.

"Why did you kill him?" he was asked. He replied: "The man was a gang leader, and his co-commander was the police inspector, with whom he shared his loot. I had been a victim of their gang's outrages and I did not want to lend myself to the criminal acts that they proposed to me; so then, in collusion with the police inspector, the gang had charges filed against me for an *ammonizione*. When I left the court-room I lost my head, bought a pistol and killed him. And, if you want proof of what I'm telling you, go to the dead man's house right now and you'll find written proof." The Carabinieri went, and they found letters and documents proving the existence of the criminal organization and demonstrating the total criminal guilt of both the gangsters and the public-safety officials.

I will cite another case for you in which the same police officer was involved. At that time a group of counterfeiters was operating unhindered and no one had been able to uncover it.* On one occasion the National Bank was informed that a shipment of specially made paper for the forgers' use was en route from Paris to Catania. One of the bank's own employees saw the shipment arrive in the post office, and two guards were posted for the purpose of arresting whoever came to take delivery of it. But this precaution did no good; the criminal managed mysteriously to remove the package without being arrested. Later it became known that the counterfeit gang could not be exposed because the inspector who had been assigned to investigate it was a member of it.

HONORABLE GATTORNO: But these statements belong to another world!

DE FELICE GIUFFRIDA: Do you suppose this inspector was turned over to the courts? The then Premier promised that the criminal would be punished in a manner that would serve as a lesson. And the inspector was in fact removed from his post, but, under an order that

---

*One of its members, before he fled to the United States, was Giuseppe Morello.—Author.

was issued very soon afterward, he was appointed superintendent of the Catania prison.

So the traditions are kept alive: the public-safety officials of those days are just like those of today, who go before the Court of Assizes in Milan to testify in the trial for the murder of Emanuele di Notarbartolo, the director of the Bank of Sicily.

And you saw—in the face of a Mafia action of such gravity, the murder of a man who enjoyed the esteem of the public, at a trial that had aroused so much indignation—you saw officials of the public-safety forces go into the Court of Assizes without any hesitation about refusing to talk; lying, concealing; you saw officials who took transcripts and reports that accused the heads of the Mafia and turned them over to the very same persons whom they denounced. You saw high officials admit that they had not taken any action whatever when they learned that the reports they had sent to the judicial authorities had mysteriously been lost in transit.

But, what is even more serious, some members of the public-safety forces were publicly accused of having concealed the blood-stained socks that could have been evidence of the murder, and no one gave a thought to at least suspending them from duty.

And now I will go on to the third level of this criminal association that is called the Mafia: the powerful, the gentry, the politicians.

I shall be more concise, honorable colleagues, more precise, more composed, if that is possible, because the violence in this third part of my statement comes from the very utterance of the facts. And, as I begin to discuss the roles played by the powerful, the gentry, and the politicians in the manifestations of this criminal phenomenon, I should like to recall a few words from a letter that a respected professor wrote to me from Palermo. Among other things, he assures me that he had heard from a senior official of the police "that the public-safety forces' hands are tied by the *top Mafia* and by the deputies who are members of it." (Lively reactions.)

THE PRESIDENT: But, my honorable colleague—

DE FELICE GIUFFRIDA: Indeed, it is well that you hear what else this eminent professor told me: he wrote to me that "a deputy (whose name I have ascertained) remarked in a conversation with a senior public-safety official: 'In the end, the Mafia is an institution that must be respected.' "

VOICES: Who was he? Give us his name.

DE FELICE GIUFFRIDA: Shall I reveal it?

A DEPUTY: You have to reveal it; we are all being accused.

DE FELICE GIUFFRIDA: Mr. President, if you authorize me to reveal it, I will.

VOICES: Yes, yes.

THE PRESIDENT: You are reading from private letters, and this is not the place in which to present outsiders' opinions.

DE FELICE GIUFFRIDA: Inasmuch as the President will not permit me to mention that deputy's name and since the Chamber, on the other hand, insists that I mention it, I will bow to the President's ruling and, as soon as I have finished speaking, I will show the name to him only.

VOICES: No, no. Tell it now.

DE FELICE GIUFFRIDA: Furthermore, my honored colleagues, you ought to know, before you begin to shout, that there is information yet to come that will make you shout even louder. And that is the certainty of the conviction that all this could not really be the work of only one deputy*—this maintenance of an organization so huge that its reach extends not only into the rural areas of the Province of Palermo but into the private office of the Police Commissioner of that city and into the staffs of the nation's Ministers.

A still more serious phenomenon, in my opinion, my honored colleagues, is this: as soon as any public-safety official indicated that he was about to act, he was immediately transferred.

I defy anyone to make a liar of me!

And who ordered those transfers? This time the name will have to come from the Premier.

PREMIER PELLOUX: What are you saying?

DE FELICE GIUFFRIDA: As soon as Sighele, a public prosecutor, indicated that he intended to proceed in earnest, he was immediately ordered to leave Palermo. As soon as another official, Trasselli, an appeals and indictment counselor, attempted to put his finger on the source of the problems, he was not only transferred but also, I have been reliably told, intimidated.

Who procured these transfers? Who made these threats? Only the government can know the answer and ought to give it; because

---

*De Felice Giuffrida was alluding to Raffaele Palizzolo who, at the moment, was in custody on the charge of having commissioned the murder of Marquis Emanuele di Notarbartolo, director of the Bank of Sicily.—Author.

all those who are deputies from Sicily, and who were shouting at me a moment ago to mention names, have an imperative right to know, indeed need to know in whose interest it could have been to hide the truth.

VOICES: Bravo! Hear, hear!

DE FELICE GIUFFRIDA: For that matter, gentlemen, we know very well that the Mafia is a necessity for many deputies in Sicily (Laughter.)

THE PRESIDENT: Honorable De Felice!

DE FELICE GIUFFRIDA: Would you want me any calmer and quieter than this?

THE PRESIDENT: I am calling you to order. It is not permissible to speak of the Chamber in this fashion!

DE FELICE GIUFFRIDA: I am merely setting forth a fact that is well known to the Chamber and to the country, and I might add that, because of the lack of time and opportunity, I am saying much less than I could tell. Is it not true, moreover, that in many districts it is the Mafia that runs the elections?

Disprove it if you can!

Is it not true that in the district that he represents—and it pains me to speak of him, who is now the most directly involved—the Honorable Palizzolo need not set up committees because there is a secret committee that pushes his candidacy and this committee is the Mafia?

Is it not true that in many other districts the Mafia has provided the constituency for candidates supported by the government? The Mafia does something further: it increases the credit of those political leaders who enjoy any; it misappropriates municipal funds, it misappropriates the funds of charitable organizations, it steals money from the public treasury. It also performs a further function: it assists in the disappearance of men who are wanted or to whom the secret of some crime has been entrusted.

On the subject of keepers of secrets whose disappearances have been facilitated, would the Honorable Premier be able to tell us anything about the disappearance of the four members of the Mafia who had indicated a desire to submit confessions in the Notarbartolo murder? I am speaking of four witnesses: Tuttilmondo, the baker, Dalma, the tavern keeper, and Lo Porto and Caruso, the coachmen, all of whom were said to have gone to America to seek their fortunes. The truth is that they were done away with to prevent their damaging the fortunes of certain kid-glove Mafiosi! Could the Honorable Premier tell us something about them? For the news must have reached even him that the bodies of those four poor devils were found in a cave near Palermo.

This is what the Mafia can be useful for. And it can also be useful to help people flee when they have been publicly accused, people like Giuseppe Fontana,* for example, who, it appears, was proved to be the real killer of Notarbartolo. He should have been watched, at least, by the police. Instead he was allowed to flee!

HONORABLE BERTESI: They should have watched him at least as closely as they do a Socialist deputy! (Laughter.)

DE FELICE GIUFFRIDA: But what is more serious is the fact that every so often the government takes the trouble to establish this benevolent association in places where the Mafia does not yet exist. (Shouts.)

This is a fact!

In the latest elections, in one district in the Province of Catania —simply to take one example—they needed a dozen Mafiosi. (Laughter.) Since, as you know, such things do not exist in Catania, just as they do not exist in Messina and Siracusa, some really big Mafiosi were sent for from where they were in compulsory residence; they were armed, they were paid two hundred lire apiece, they were booked into a previously chosen hotel where they could eat and amuse themselves, and they kept themselves available to public safety forces to threaten, to intimidate, and to act in the interests of an Under-Secretary of State. (Various remarks.)

If, honored colleagues, what I am saying seems exaggerated to you, you can apply for proof to a conservative deputy, the Honorable Aprile, who is better qualified to describe other matters to you. The deputy from San Giuliano himself could tell you something about them if he wished. (Laughter.)

Bt that as it may, it is certain that the Mafia carries on its criminal activities with the help of the government. I myself was confronted one day by four Mafiosi who had been commissioned to pay me one of their customary compliments. I did not seek help from the public authorities—that would have been a waste of breath!

---

*The speaker meant the Black Hand member in New York, a friend of Giuseppe Morello.—Author.

But, knowing the Mafiosi, I faced all four of them and, with the backing of a friend who had given more than ample evidence of his courage at Domokos, I said to them: "What do you want? Here I am."

As for the police, they simply allowed them to follow us and ambush us. This is serious. I should like to mention another person, who, after having received an *ammonizione* and been sentenced to compulsory residence, was still available to certain friends in the government.

One day this fellow made some threats to friends of mine. "Listen," I said to him, "just remember I know how to put you in your place even if you do have the police on your side!" And that wretch replied: "What did I do wrong? I've had the *ammonizione,* I've been ordered into compulsory residence, but I can stay here. I have freedom, money, and protection—I have everything. Why should I jeopardize all that?"

No one can deny that, when it is election time, the most dangerous offenders are relieved of the restrictions of the *ammonizione,* the most shady individuals are released from compulsory residence, permission to carry weapons is granted to known ruffians; and all this in order to be able to exert pressure on political opponents through the pressures and threats of these scoundrels, placed at the disposal of the government candidate. Let anyone deny it if he has the courage!

Tell me, is it not therefore the government that furthers the growth of the Mafia where it already exists and that invites its inception where it does not exist?

I have spoken at length, gentlemen, and therefore I will not offer opinions. Besides, the facts are more eloquent than any opinions. For me, then, there is nothing more to do but to wait for Parliament to adopt those measures that are required to strike down not the small fry, the unfortunate, the victims, but those who are at the top, though they wear the uniforms of officers or of ordinary policemen, though they boast the honors bestowed by the Crown of Italy! (Applause from the extreme Left.)

Giuseppe De Felice Giuffrida's panoramic depiction of the collusion between Mafiosi and politicians was in no way exaggerated. The deputy could in fact have added that there were politicians who actually assumed kinship (through blood-brotherhood rituals) with illiterate Mafia leaders simply in order to be elected, and others who kissed the Mafiosi's hands in the public squares, and still others (among them a future Premier) who did not hesitate, during election campaigns, to put up posters reading: "Vote for X, the friend of the friends."

One of the most troublesome figures of that era was the Honorable Palizzolo, to whom De Felice Giuffrida alluded several times in his speech. Don Raffaele, as everyone called Palizzolo in Palermo, was the best known and the most influential of the politically active Mafiosi on the island. Very closely linked with Crispi and later with di Rudinì, he controlled every seat of power in western Sicily. He was simultaneously a deputy in Parliament, a municipal and provincial councilor in Palermo, the chairman of a dozen charitable organizations, a member of the board of directors of the Bank of Sicily, and the major stockholder in the Navigation Company. At the beginning of the final decade of the nineteenth century, which was marked by a series of banking scandals that rocked "the honest Italy of Umberto," Palizzolo had succeeded in engineering the ouster of the Marquis di Notarbartolo, an upright, able man, from the management of the Bank of Sicily in order to replace him with the Duca della Verdura, with whom Palizzolo had political and economic ties. Having become virtually the monarch of the bank, Palizzolo embarked on a series of operations and speculations of such a nature as to threaten the bank with a major crisis.

Emanuele Notarbartolo, who had of course not taken kindly to his unjust ouster, attempted to expose the climate of shady dealings and sharp practices that had developed in the bank; he sent a report to Miceli, the Minister of Finance. We do not know what the ingenuous marquis expected from this revelation, but the result was that Miceli forwarded the report to Crispi and Crispi gave it to Palizzolo. The whole thing ended there.

Notarbartolo, however, made another attempt when Crispi's government fell and Giolitti came to power. This time, however, the situation at once turned delicate; it was announced that there would be an inquiry, in which, obviously, Notarbartolo would be the major figure.

But the trusting marquis never had time to carry his work through to its conclusion. On February 1, 1893 he was murdered, stabbed twenty-seven times, in a first-class compartment of a train on the line between Termini and Palermo; specifically in the stretch between Trabia and Altavilla.

That this was a Mafia crime no one doubted. Nevertheless the case dragged on inconclusively for years. And there were disturbing elements: everyone knew and mentioned the killers' names, but not a single police official paid any attention. Notarbartolo's son, who was an officer in the navy and who very naturally was making every effort to have justice done, was assigned to duty in the China Sea (he would later have to go on leave in order to pursue the matter). Palizzolo, meanwhile, in the midst of public accusations of responsibility for the murder, was awarded a decoration for his *civic virtues* by King Umberto. Everyone, in Rome and in Palermo, conspired to bury the business.

Finally, if most laboriously, there was progress. The first step was the arrest of a group of Mafiosi from Villabate, among them the notorious Giuseppe Fontana. They were accused of having actually carried out the murder, but their trial ended in an acquittal. Subsequently, as a result of pressure by Notarbartolo's son, there was a second trial in Milan in which the principal defendant was Giuseppe Fontana. But during the course of the trial, such strong evidence against Palizzolo emerged that the Chamber (whose President then was the Piedmontese Pelloux) did not hesitate to grant authorization to proceed against him.

Don Raffaele was arrested on December 8, 1899. Although every merchant in Palermo closed his business out of "civic mourning," the arrest was upheld.

The first trial was held in Bologna, running from September 1901 to July 1902, and it ended with the sentencing of Raffaele Palizzolo and Giuseppe Fontana to prison. The verdict and sentence were overthrown on appeal, however, so a second trial was begun in Florence in September of 1903.

In the intervening ten years since the crime various witnesses had died (naturally and otherwise); others had emigrated; still others had "lost their memories." In short, on July 25, 1904 the Florence jury acquitted Palizzolo and Fontana for lack of evidence. The relase of Palizzolo created a sensation. While the mainland newspapers, and particularly *Avanti!*,* analyzed the outcome of the Florence trial in bewilderment, all Palermo was on holiday. The steamer Malta was chartered to sail for Naples to bring Palizzolo home; the procession in honor of the Madonna del Carmine was postponed to enable the former jailbird to take part; the members of the Florence jury were proclaimed honorary citizens of Palermo; The Honorable Di Stefano, who had succeeded Palizzolo as a deputy, resigned his seat in favor of his predecessor.

The police authorities whom De Felice Giuffrida had openly accused of colluding with the Mafia and of concealing evidence damaging to Palizzolo were the same men from whom the head of the Italian Legion of the New York police force expected serious collaboration in his battle against the Italian underworld in America. But Petrosino could not have known the truth about the Mafia's position in Sicily, nor could he have known that, even as they were officially promising their attention to the matter, the Italian authorities were undermining the American effort. The Italian government was issuing secret instructions to its officials to ensure their advising and furthering emigration to America of those subject to *ammonizioni,* those under special surveillance or released from prison. Hence Petrosino did not know that for any criminal in Italy it was the easiest thing in the world to obtain a passport and a clean police record. And, in the event that, for one reason or another, legal means did not suffice, there was always Duke Francesco di Villarosa in Palermo who, on receipt of the sum of five hundred lire, would provide any kind of document to anyone who asked for it.

*The official newspaper of the Socialist Party.—Translator.

7. Don Vito Cascio Ferro

IT IS SAID THAT VITO CASCIO FERRO, when he returned to Italy from the United States in his flight from prosecution for the "barrel murder," took with him a photograph of Joseph Petrosino. "I who have never been tained by a crime," he would tell his friends (according to the tale), as he showed them the policeman's picture, "I swear that I will kill this man with my own hands."

The pledge is apocryphal. The fact of the photograph, however, has been verified: Don Vito did indeed keep it in his wallet, in the manner of the American killers who always want to be absolutely sure that they are not firing at the wrong target.

Vito Carscio Ferro was born in Palermo on January 22, 1862. His father, Accursio, was a "follower" of the baronial Inglese family, along with whom he had moved to Bisaquino, near Palermo, in order to manage the Ingleses' farm at Santa Maria del Bosco.

Vito never went to school, but he did learn to read and write. When he was still very young he married the village school teacher, Brigida Giaccone, who not only brought as her dowry the house in which the couple would live, but also taught her bridegroom the fundamentals of literacy. He was a tall, quite attractive man whose face was framed in a short, well-cared-for blond beard. He dressed with a certain elegance—like a gentleman, as they said in those times; he smoked very-long-stemmed pipes and gave off that aura of authority that in Sicily marks "men of respect." Almost unconsciously the peasants fonnd themselves obeying him and prefacing his name with the honorific *Don.*

Working did not seem to arouse much interest in Don Vito. He was vaguely involved in certain buying and selling for one of the Barons Inglese and in some undefined kind of representation of the Caruso public-transit interests. He preferred, however, to spend his time in the bars and taverns of Bisaquino and Palermo, manifesting particular interest in the game of *giusso,* a kind of Sicilian-style poker.

Later, when the wave of anarchism began to sweep over the island, Don Vito was one of the first to join the movement. His was an ebullient temperament; he liked to settle disputes, play the peacemaker, redress wrongs, employ the influence of his personality, bring everyone under his protective wing. In sum, he had all the standard characteristics of the potential Mafioso. But in the beginning he was an anarchist, and as such he undertook much activity. He was president of the Fasci of Bisaquino in 1892, he took part in the seizures of estates, and, after the harsh repressions ordered by Crispi, he went into hiding in Tunisia for about a year in order to avoid being placed in compulsory residence. This youthful excess was never disowned by Vito Cascio Ferro. Rather strangely, he was to go on viewing himself as a friend of the people and a man of the Left even when he had become the most important Mafia leader of all time.

On his return from Tunisia, however, Don Vito gave up politics in order to devote himself to more profitable ventures. It was certainly at this period that he organized his first criminal gang, but information about him is scarce. One can only theorize, as did the chief public safety official in Bisquino. "It is believed," he wrote to the Police Commissioner of Palermo, "that the well-known Vito Cascio Ferro is behind the robbery of three merchants whose carriage was stopped by an unknown man who identified himself as the director of public safety." And again: "It is supposed that the priest armed with a rifle who attacked the large Lo Bianco farm was the notorious Vito Cascio Ferro, skillfully disguised . . ."

The offenses definitively charged to Don Vito in those years and recorded in his police files are those of attacks against property, arson and disrespect for public officials, but here, obviously, we are dealing with acts that occurred during the peasant protest movements. One must, indeed, move on to 1898 in order to catch Don Vito, as the saying goes, in the act. The incident in which the already influential resident of Bisaquino became a major character is in some aspects still rather unclear today.

On the evening of June 13 the nineteen-year-old Baroness Clorinda Peritelli di Valpetroso was abducted by three persons as she was riding in her carriage along Via Paolo Paternostro in Palermo. At first the girl was taken to a house in the country, where a woman whom she described as "kind" stayed with her all night. Then she was set free the next day, presumably because her parents had delivered the ransom.

The police, however, had not been sitting on their hands. As a result of information from informers, they were at length able to lay their hands on the suspected abductors, whom Baroness Clorinda did not hesitate to identify when she was called to police headquarters. They were Vito Cascio Ferro, a student named Girolamo Campisi, Giusto Picone, Antonio Enea, Pietro di Benedetto, Valentino di Leo and Lucrezia Zerbo. Things looked very bad for the whole gang; but Don Vito was not the kind to give up so easily. He asserted that the case was one of *abduction for love:* Campisi, the student, who was madly in love with the beautiful Clorinda, had implored him to lend his assistance and he, Don Vito, being at bottom a romantic, had not had the will to refuse.

It is not known precisely how things proceeded, but apparently Don Vito's version was accepted by everyone (even though, as the official transcripts show, the kidnapped Clorinda resolutely denied ever having had any kind of contact with Campisi). So Don Vito was given only a three-year suspended sentence. The other defendants were also allowed to go home in peace.

As a consequence of this affair, nevertheless, proceedings for an *ammonizione* were initiated against the former anarchist, and soon afterward he decided to leave the country. Having bidden farewell to his wife without too much pain—by now she was fatalistically resigned to her restless consort's strange behavior—and acquired a proper passport and certificate of good character from the local police, he arrived in Marseilles early in August 1901 and boarded a ship for the United States.

In New York he lived for a while on Twenty-third Street with his sister Francesca, who was the wife of Salvatore Armato. Then he acquired a place of his own at 117 Morgan Street. From the earliest days of his residence in the United States, Don Vito became an important personage in Sicilian-American criminal circles; his reputation had preceded him and his intelligence and authoritative manner did the rest.

Furthermore, he was the first Mafioso "of respect" to set foot in the country, and hence it was natural that everyone should already look on him as the future head of the honorable society. It ought also to be noted that his entrance into the underworld did not cause frictions of any kind with the local bosses. No one was his equal, and the various subchiefs of gangs, such as Morello, Lupo, Fontana, who in Sicily had acted as mere cut-throats or, in any case, lower-level leaders, at once reacted to Don Vito with that mixture of veneration and fear that small fry always feel toward born commanders.

One illustration of the deferential reception that awaited Don Vito upon landing in New York is to be found in a letter that was addressed to him at the time and that was later found among his papers:

New York, 12 September 1901
My very dear Don Vito,
I welcome you and allow myself the pleasure and the liberty
of inviting you to my home. I have also taken the liberty of inviting friends, Giuseppe Morello, Francesco Megna, Giuseppe
Fontana, Carlo Costantino, and Gioacchino di Martino to eat a
platter of macaroni together. We thought that next Monday
would be good and that the best time might be three o'clock in
the afternoon. I hope that you will not fail to come, and, if the
day and the time are not convenient for you, let me know by
messenger.
I kiss your hand.

Your
Salvatore Brancaccio

In the few years that he spent in the United States, Don Vito
was unquestionably the grey eminence of the Black Hand, whose
methods he reorganized so that they became more efficient and
more productive. It is certain that he had contacts with the
anarchist movement as well; he had not forgotten that he had been
a member of it. He went frequently to Paterson, where he was
greeted as a "veteran of the glorious Sicilian risings of '92," and
where he created the impression that he had left Italy for political
reasons. He even asked to be introduced to the former Sophie
Knieland, Gaetano Bresci's widow, who had moved to Cliffside
with her daughter Madeleine. They became friends and often exchanged letters.

One cannot know what Don Vito had in mind in seeking to
establish relations with the anarchists, who at that time had a
considerable following in the United States. Nor do we know what
were his long-range plans; if he had any (and surely he did),
they were thwarted by Joe Petrosino's arrival on the scene.

The facts are known. After the "barrel murder," Don Vito attempted first of all to throw off the police investigation (the
clever device of impersonating the killer was the product of his

imagination), and then he fled to New Orleans, where he remained for about a year as the guest of trusted friends.

By now America was no longer a hospitable country for Don Vito. The charges brought against him by Petrosino had also blocked his application for citizenship. Had he wanted to stay, he would have had to resign himself to living under a false name, a prospect that did not entice him. Consequently he decided to go back to Italy.

He sailed out of New Orleans on September 28, 1904, carrying a telegram that had reached him that same day from New York: "Much alarmed your troubles. Don't worry about me and others. We hope you find everything all right. Good luck. Write when arrive. Giuseppe." The sender was probably Giuseppe Morello.

On his return to Palermo, Don Vito realized that, while he had been in some danger before, all trace of it was gone by now. Everyone he knew greeted him with the old deference.

His first task was to establish an organizational structure for the Palermo-New York circuit, which until then had consisted of relations between persons rather than between groups. Because of his influence both in Sicily and in America, Don Vito very quickly became the pivot in the alliance between two criminal associations: the Mafia and the Black Hand. In a word, it was he who created the vast empire of crime, with permanent, solid interconnections, that exists today and that comes out into the open every now and then when the newspapers disclose that the Mafiosi on both sides of the ocean have equal power and influence in the management of specific illegal operations.

This bold enterprise substantially enhanced the power of the former subversive from Bisaquino. He was now forty-two years old; his face had become more impressive and his beard, with its threads of white here and there, was more imposing. It was in this period that Don Vito's star soared to the highest points in the Mafia firmament.

Demonstrating his great capacities, in less than two years he succeeded in gaining control of all the Mafia branches in the area.

According to a police report, he was simultaneously the head of the Mafia of Bisaquino, Palermo, Burgio, Corleone, Campofiorito, Contessa, Estellina, Chiusa, Sclafani, Sciacca, Sambuca Zabut, and Villafranca Sicula. This was something unique in the history of Sicilian crime.

Furthermore, Don Vito was unquestionably endowed with a superior intelligence. A superb organizer, a true industrialist of crime, he inaugurated the fiscal system of *protection* in his fief with such a sense of justice that many of his victims complimented him on it. He found it difficult to read, but he was capable of reckoning to the penny the earnings of any merchant on whom he had decided to levy a fair tax. He was the first to revise the primitive pastoral methods of the peasant Mafia to fit the complicated conditions of the modern city. He organized all the various criminal crafts, and even the beggars were assigned to individual beats.

Naturally, as often happens in Sicily with persons of this sort, the legend has frequently blurred the truth, and even today people like to think of Don Vito as a kind of gentleman-brigand always ready for the fine gesture. They tend, however, to forget the hundred or so persons (at least) that he had disposed of by his killers.

In those days he divided his time between Bisaquino and Palermo, where he lodged (free) in the city's best hotels. His favorites were the Albergo Pizzuto in Via Bandiera and the Hôtel de France in Piazza Marina. For lunch he customarily went to the Cafè Oreto when not dining at the home of one of his eminent Palermo friends. In addition to his close ties with Barons Salvatore and Antonino Inglese, he had become the confidential agent of the Honorable Domenico De Michele Ferrantelli, a deputy from Bivona. To call him a *confidential agent* is perhaps somewhat disrespectful to Don Vito's memory. In order to understand what their relationship actually was, one must bear in mind certain subtleties. When, for instance, the two men together toured the various towns in the district during an election campaign, the mayors in their tricolor sashes would hurry to the entrances of their towns to kiss Don Vito's hand. The Honorable De Michele's hand they were satisfied to shake.

In order to gain some further idea of the distance that Vito
Cascio Ferro traveled after his return from the United States, it is
worth studying the two reports that follow. They were sent by the
local prefect to the Minister of the Interior. It should be noted
that the interval between them was exactly ten years, but the same
man was the author of both.

10 May 1898

Prefecture of Palermo
Subject: Cascio Ferro, Vito; father, Accursio; mother, the late
Santa Ippolito; born in Palermo 22 January 1862; residing
in Bisaquino; no property; agent; husband of Brigida Giac-
cone, elementary school teacher; no children.
Official Description:
Height: tall
Build: rather slender
Hair: chestnut
Forehead: average
Nose: pointed, with wide nostrils
Eyes: large, brown
Mouth: rather wide
Chin: round
Face: thin
Complexion: slightly pale
Beard: shaped to a point, Mephistophelian
Bearing: arrogant
Facial expression: Mafioso
Usual dress: civilian
Special characteristics: none
Biographical Details: He is held in the lowest regard by respect-
able citizens, who consider him a very dangerous individual
from every point of view; whereas he is held in high esteem
and respect by Mafiosi and Socialists.

He has a limited education, great intelligence, little or no cul-
ture, and it is not known how far he went in school since he has
no academic certificates. He is given to idleness, gambling and
debauchery. His means of support are his wife's salary and what
he earns as a representative of the Caruso road-transport firm; but
these would not be sufficient because he dresses well and fre-

quently goes to Palermo and stays there for long periods in a style from which it is to be deduced that he has other and illegal sources of income. In the past he spent his time exclusively in the company of Mafiosi, criminals and Socialists, but for some time he has been going to the Civilian Club of Bisaquino, where he is reluctantly tolerated. In his obligations to his family he is delinquent, inasmuch as he often abuses and beats his wife with a stick. He has never held any political or administrative post. He is enrolled in the Socialist Revolutionary Party and has great influence not only in this town but also in Burgio, Sambuca Zabut, Sciacca, and Corleone, and he maintains continuing relations with leaders and comrades, often going to visit them in those places.

From December 1893 to September 1894 he lived in Tunis, to which he had fled after the proclamation of the state of siege in Sicily, in order to avoid being subjected to compulsory residence. He returned to this country voluntarily, promising the Police Commissioner that he would never again engage in political activity. He is a member of the Workers' Fascio of Bisaquino, of which he is also president; his behavior is bold, violent and full of outspoken incitements to destruction. He does not now collaborate and never has collaborated in any journalistic work. He receives subversive publications in the mail, which he picks up in person on his frequent journeys to Palermo.

He has engaged in extremely active propaganda among the peasants, to whom he has preached that property is theft, and by whom he is held in the highest regard, so much so that they declare themselves prepared to obey him and to follow him at the slightest sign from him. At the time of the Fasci he made various clandestine speeches to the great profit of his party, and—a thing that seems incredible in view of the character, the educaion and the natural endowment of this agricultural class—prevailed on the women to stop going to Holy Communion and to come instead and make their confessions to him and to the other leaders of the Fascio. He has always behaved with contempt toward the authorities. He has never been held for or subjected to judicial *ammonizione.* He was to have been placed in compulsory residence in 1894 but the order could not be executed because he fled to Tunis.

Many and fearsome are the crimes that public opinion attributes to Vito Cascio Ferro, but on his police record there appear only a few fines for misdemeanors, whereas he has always been acquitted of criminal arson and disrespect to the public authorities.

The Prefect

Prefecture of Palermo, 12 May 1908
Subject: Cascio Ferro, Vito, son of Accursio
This Royal Prefecture is informed that the subject individual, who in the past professed subversive principles, has renounced his former political comrades since 1900 and has conducted himself irreproachably. He has now formed new and legitimate friendships with Baron Inglese and the Honorable De Michele Ferranti, both of whom have the utmost confidence in him. He enjoys the esteem of all honest citizens, to such a degree that he has been accepted as a member of the Civilian Club; he enjoys the best relations with the gentry and, above all, he has shown himself to be respectful toward the Authorities.

De Seta, Prefect

After his return from America Don Vito became a "man of *great* respect." He bought his clothes at Bustarino's, the shop in Via Maqueda that was famous in those days because it provided its customers with the cream of the English market; he went to the theater and he mingled with the best society. Many people would have been astounded to learn that this elegant gentleman was a semiliterate peasant and that beneath his English suit he still wore the big belt with a series of notches cut into it that he utilized in figuring his accounts, as if it were an abacus.

At any event, they all knew that he was important. Whether out of self-interest or out of fear, or even out of spontaneous admiration, they competed with one another to become his friends.

"Lucky the man who kisses your hand, Don Vito," they would greet him. And he, very graciously, offered his hand to everyone, even to the authorities, to be kissed. As a real Mafioso he took good care, above all, to win people's respect. In a certain sense he loved power more than money. And in all honesty, he was never greedy; he took pleasure rather in having friends always ready to place at his disposal whatever sum he might need.

The halo that surrounded him was one of mystery as well as of respect, and the ordinary populace did not hesitate to link his name with certain colorful legends (such as that of the Blessed Pauls, a seventeenth-century penitential order that some would like to establish as the ancestor of the earliest Mafia). Indeed, it seems that he did concern himself greatly with the revival of the ancient rites of the Mafia, organizing complicated ceremonials of investiture and theatrical trials in which the fates of dangerous enemies or of members suspected of treachery were decided in gloomy, gruesome settings.

It may seem strange that Don Vito, a practical, modern Mafioso, should have loved this kind of theatricality. But the rumors that circulated on the subject appear to be corroborated by the curious report that was submitted by the chief of public safety for Bisaquino, Cavalier Ponzi, in August 1908 to the Police Commissioner of Palermo, Baldassare Ceola.

In the course of the investigations into the activities of the notorious Cascio Ferro, Vito, I was told that for some time he has been a member of a criminal association in Palermo, and, by way of evidence, I was told that some time ago the same Cascio Ferro instructed a person from Bisaquino to deliver a letter to a house adjoining a church close to the municipal pawnshop in Palermo, which house is reached by a rather small door alongside the said church, which door, at a knock, would be opened to the messenger by a young female deaf-mute, who, having accepted the letter, would open a smaller door leading to a cellar and from there would return with a letter of reply, containing money, which she would hand over to him.

The messenger, having found the house described to him, followed the instructions given to him, and, when he had delivered the letter, the deaf-mute, probably the sister of the sacristan of the said church, whose home he believed the said house to be, having opened the door leading to the cellar, which it seemed to him extended under the aforesaid church, ushered him into it.

There he found together a number of individuals unknown to him and dangerous in appearance; and some tables arranged in regular order convinced him that this was the meeting place of the criminals, where the distribution of their booty took place and where sentences on the members were pronounced. When he had waited for some time, the letter of reply with money for the addressee was handed to him, and, before he left, it was borne in on him that, on pain of death in the event of disobedience, he must keep the secret of what he had seen.

Assiduous search having therefore been made in order to identify the mysterious house, I have been compelled to the conviction that the church in question is that of the Blessed Pauls, situated in the square of the same name, and the house above-described is that adjoining the said church and situated at the exact point at which the square in question forms a corner with the Orphans' Lane.

It must also be pointed out, however, that the report by the punctilious official in Bisaquino offers no opportunity for any kind of verification; therefore, in the final analysis, the existence of this curious gathering-place remains shrouded in doubt.

7. "We'll Have to Go It Alone"

IN AN OUTBURST OF IRRITATION Joseph Petrosino tossed his derby onto the nearest chair and planted himself in front of Commissioner Bingham's desk.

"General," he said, "I'm fed up with working to no end. All the deportation proceedings initiated by the department have been thrown out again by the courts. And do you know what reasons they gave?" Commissioner Bingham merely shrugged. "One case was dismissed because the deportee's description was not just right; another because the man has lived in America three years and five days (as if we were the ones who had kept postponing the case month after month!); a third because no one knows what port he sailed here from and so they can't decide where to deport him to. Shall I go on?"

"No, that's enough," Bingham replied, sighing. "By now I know the story backward."

But Petrosino went on anyway. "Do you know what a year's work in this field comes down to? Out of five thousand Italian criminals tracked down and listed by my squad, we've managed to get orders for exactly twenty to be thrown out of the country. And seven of those twenty mysteriously succeeded in escaping from Ellis Island just before they were due to sail."

"Lieutenant," Bingham said, "you're right. Unfortunately our laws are what they are. Nevertheless, what we've lacked most has been the cooperation of the Italian police."

"So? Does that mean we have to resign ourselves?"

"Not by any means." The police commissioner's voice had suddenly turned harsh. "But, as I've already told you so often, we'll have to go it alone."

The detective looked at his superior in bewilderment. Bingham had been making that same observation for some time. "What do you mean by *alone,* General?"

"I'll explain it to you in due course, Lieutenant. It's an idea of mine and it may produce substantial results. The matter is under study now, and you'll be pleased to know that you are to have a very important part in the execution of my plan."

By the spring of 1908, about a year after its passage by the Senate, the new American immigration law had already been proved a total failure. The lawyers for criminals threatened with deportation orders knew countless ways to invalidate or to get around almost every provision in the statute.

Taking cognizance of the ineffectiveness of the legislation, the American Congress, acting at the suggestion of the President himself, appointed a number of committees of both Senators and Representatives to go to Europe and, in particular, to Italy to investigate the situation on the spot, with a view to a new law that might prove adequate to keep criminals out of the country.

One of these committees had even been received by King Vittorio

Emanuele III who pledged his personal cooperation but very carefully confined himself to generalities. Senator Latimer of South Carolina had introduced a bill under which every would-be immigrant to the United States would have to produce a "certificate of origin" issued by the American consulate nearest to his place of residence.

These Congressional committees' trips to Europe cost the United States Treasury about three-hundred-thousand dollars, but their practical results may be deduced from a comment by *The New York Times,* which said: "In view of the fact that the influx into our country of the rabble of Naples, Calabria and Sicily is reaching its peak, the efforts of our senators may be likened to those of the shepherd who, while the wolves were pillaging his sheepfold, ran to the library to consult a text on zoology."

Almost as if by deliberate plan, Raffaele Palizzolo, the deputy who had been sentenced to prison in the murder of Marquis Emanuele di Notarbartolo, decided to make a journey to the United States just when the controversy over the Italian underworld was attaining new intensity. The reasons for the visit were purely political. Palizzolo intended to run as a candidate from the Palermo district in the elections scheduled for March 1, 1909, and he had thought up this visit to the Sicilian colony in the United States both for its propaganda effect at home and for the solicitation of campaign funds. In fact, his baggage included some twenty thousand copies of an autobiographical work called *Le mie prigioni* (*My Prisons*) that he proposed to offer to his admirers at a dollar apiece.

The former deputy arrived in New York on June 8, 1908, on board the liner *Martha Washington.* He was accompanied by a cousin named Ferlazzo who was a lawyer and the editor and publisher of a Palermo newspaper, *La Forbice* (*The Scissors*).

Unbelievable though it may seem, this notorious representative of the Mafia who, it will be recalled, was at this time no longer a deputy was given an official welcome. As a result of a well-planned press campaign carried out by *Il Progresso italo-americano* and some other small Italian-language newspapers, thousands of

Sicilians, wearing what has now become the conventional "button" (though for those days it was a great novelty) with Palizzolo's picture on it, had flocked to the pier. At the head of the cheering crowd stood the Italian Consul General in New York, Count Massiglia, who introduced the visitor to the American authorities as an "official representative of the Italian government" dispatched to the United States to conduct an educational campaign among the Sicilians and to combat the "Black Hand" and the Mafia.

Even more incredibly, these statements by the Consul General were accepted as gospel truth. Commissioner Bingham himself told *The New York Times* that same day: "I am certain that the Honorable Mr. Palizzolo will be able to offer valuable help to the New York police in their fight against the 'Black Hand.'"

But Palizzolo's face could not be kept up very long. A courageous newspaper, *Il Bollettino della Sera* (*The Evening Bulletin*), resolved to tell Italians in the United States just what was the character of this man who had taken it upon himself to educate the Sicilians. Other Italian newspapers followed its example, but *Il Progresso,* backed up by the influential *New York Herald* and its Italian subsidiary, *l'Araldo,* proceeded unperturbed in its advocacy of Palizzolo.

This created a division among Italians. In many of the cities that he visited, Palizzolo found himself ignored, but in others, on the contrary, he was extravagantly welcomed. His great successes, of course, occurred where there were the most Sicilians. Some newspapers also reported that the former deputy had had a number of meetings with his *friend* Giuseppe Fontana, "his companion in the martyrdom of the long trial," and with Giuseppe Morello and Ignazio Lupo. But, to convey some concrete notion of the enthusiasm that Palizzolo aroused in America, let me reproduce this comment on a speech that he delivered in Tammany Hall, the headquarters of the New York Democratic Party:

The true orator never chooses the wrong word. That explains how Deputy Palizzolo succeeds in rousing and influencing a crowd. Imagine this man in Piazza Quattro Cantoni, in the heart of Sezione Palazzo Reale [the Royal Palace Quarter] in Palermo, between Monte Pellegrino and Monreale: imagine him pronouncing the most sonorous, the most heated poetic prose—the only kind that is appropriate when one is speaking of Sicily—and you will understand why everyone adores the "friend of the people." You will understand the phenomenon of Palizzolo!

The "people's friend" was not destined to remain long in the United States. Having clarified matters for Commissioner Bingham, Joseph Petrosino at once began to snap at Palizzolo's heels and succeeded in breaking up more than one of his lectures, sometimes by making arrests in the audience and sometimes by raising obstacles of a bureaucratic kind. Finally the two men met face to face in Palizzolo's hotel room. No one knows what they said to each other (Petrosino never chose to reveal it, although he did let it be understood that he had "thrown some fear" into the former deputy.) Be that as it may, Raffaele Palizzolo left New York a month earlier than he had planned. He sailed on August 2, 1908, aboard the steamship Liguria. Petrosino was at the pier to watch him depart; now the detective had a new enemy in Palermo.

To allay any curiosity, I should add that the visit to America was not unprofitable for Palizzolo. He succeeded in selling out the entire stock of his book about his imprisonment and he took home the comfortable sum of twenty thousand dollars. As for the strange behavior of the Consul General of Italy, it had no serious consequences. In spite of an attack made on him in the Chamber of Deputies, Count Massiglia got off with a reprimand by the Foreign Minister and remained at his post.

Joseph Petrosino spent the rest of that summer in bed with bronchial pneumonia, which kept him out of action for a couple of months. His wife had to turn for help to a cousin much younger than herself, who was to go on living with the couple thereafter. Mrs. Petrosino, then thirty-eight, was pregnant for the first time, and there was some concern for her health.

The detective had not yet recovered when he received official notification from the Italian Consulate General that the Italian government had decided to present him with a gold watch with the following inscription over the signature of Giovanna Giolitti on its case, "With grateful recognition of brilliant work performed in the identification and arrest of criminals in flight from Italian justice." Another inscribed watch was presented to Sergeant Antonio Vachris, the head of the Italian Squad of Brooklyn.

Petrosino was not able to accept his award until October 20, when he had completely recovered, and Count Massiglia, the Consul General, presented it to him in person. Before he accepted it, however, the lieutenant had made it a point to ask official authorization to do so from Commissioner Bingham, and the letter in which he put his request is still preserved in the official records:

19 October 1908

To the Police Commissioner
New York City
Sir:

In conformance with Article 3, Chapter XXX, of the regulations of the Police Department, I respectively request permission to accept a gold watch that has been awarded to me by the Italian government.

Respectfully,
Lt. Joseph Petrosino
Chief, Italian Section
Police Headquarters

In the meantime, Commissioner Bingham had completed the private plan of which he had already spoken vaguely more than once. It was his purpose to set up in New York a secret service that would be responsible to him alone; only he would know the names of the men selected to join it; only he—without being answerable to anyone—would make all the decisions on the assignments that it would carry out.

Bingham intended to place his loyal Lieutenant Petrosino at the head of this branch, and to authorize Petrosino and his men to use every possible means, even those not sanctioned by law, "to smash the 'Black Hand' and the anarchists." In plain language, this was a project for the establishment of a police team "with permission to kill"; that is, at liberty to go after criminals without having to be concerned with the complicated requirements of the American Constitution.

When Bingham told the Board of Aldermen of his proposal, of course, he did not describe it in such bald terms. But the plan aroused fierce protest and conflict just the same. All were acutely aware of the dangers inherent in entrusting Bingham with such sweeping powers.

"You must admit," another Commissioner, Redmond, said to him during discussion of the project, "that you could turn your secret service not only against the 'Black Hand' but also in any other direction that you thought proper."

"I am Commissioner of Police," Bingham replied in authoritarian tones. "And, so long as I remain in that capacity, nobody can stop me from setting up branches as I see fit."

"We can deny you the necessary funds, however," Redmond retorted.

"I can do without your funds!" said Bingham defiantly.

The suspicions entertained by Redmond and others as to the use of the secret service "in other directions" may have been without foundation. Probably Bingham, like Petrosino, had come to the conclusion that without exceptional measures he would never uproot the poisonous weed of the Mafia, which by now was spreading throughout the state. And, in addition, the good Bingham gave full consideration to the fact that a quick, radical move against foreign criminals would guarantee him sufficient popularity to open his way to further advancement.

The fact is, in any event, that the aggressive Police Commissioner succeeded in setting up his secret service in spite of the city's decision not to appropriate the funds required. The money (approximately thirty thousand dollars for the first year's work) came from private citizens, businesses and organizations through a clandestine subscription drive. Bingham, indeed, never disclosed any names, although some newspapers identified as chief subscribers two financiers, Andrew Carnegie and John D. Rockefeller, Sr.; the City Club; the Italian Chamber of Commerce in New York; the

New York Stock Exchange; and a number of rich representatives of the Italian colony.

The official announcement of the establishment of the new organization was made in December 1908 and the spirit in which it was received by a good part of public opinion may be deduced from these headlines and subheads that the *New York Herald* ran above a four-column story:

BINGHAM'S SECRET SERVICE GETS STARTED
Elimination of "Black Hand" Is
Ostensible Purpose of
New Squad
May Have Other Uses
No One Knows Who Belongs to Special Unit
Except Its Two Chiefs
Petrosino Is Active Head
Funds for Support of Mystery Group Put
Up by Private Citizens After Refusal
by Board of Estimate*

The New York Times, however, was less suspicious than the *Herald.* The behavior of the *Herald* in this matter, as we shall see, gave rise to some question. *The Times* said:

NEW SECRET SERVICE TO BATTLE "BLACK HAND"
Police Commissioner Theodore A. Bingham finally has his Secret Service. It is secret in every sense of the word, since no one at 300 Mulberry Street except Lieutenant Petrosino and Bingham himself knows its membership.

Substantial funds for the maintenance of the Secret Squad have been made available to the Police Commissioner, but this is all that he will say. He refuses to discuss their source, confining himself to the assurance that it is not public money. It is generally believed that the money was contributed by a number of prosperous Italian merchants and bankers of the city, aroused by the wave of extortions in recent years.

---

*The Board of Aldermen was elected; the Board of Estimate consisted of the Mayor and his Commissioners and Borough Presidents, and its approval was required for all appropriations.—Translator.

It is also reported that Andrew Carnegie and John D. Rockefeller have contributed, but this has not been confirmed. When questioned on the subject, Bingham says only: "I have plenty of money, and it did not come from the city."

The members of the Secret Service have been recruited outside the Police Department and their field of operations is completely independent of it. Lieutenant Petrosino is their chief, and will be able to carry out his fight against the "Black Hand" in whatever manner he deems best. Lieutenant Petrosino's temporary successor as head of the Italian Squad is Lieutenant Gloster.

All this took place at the end of December 1908. Early in January 1909, Joseph Petrosino was informed by Bingham himself that he should get ready for a trip to Italy. Petrosino was not enthusiastic at the prospect. A few weeks earlier, on November 30, his wife had given birth to a daughter who had been baptised in St. Patrick's with the name of Adelina Bianca Giuseppina, and now, when he was almost fifty years old, Petrosino had begun to acquire a taste for family life and the joys of fatherhood. Every day, as soon as he was off duty, he hurried home to devote himself to the baby who had come into his life so late and given it a new purpose in addition to his police work.

But Petrosino was too accustomed to obeying orders to make a fuss. All that he asked was that he be kept away from home for as brief a time as possible.

The reasons that impelled Bingham to send Petrosino to Sicily have always been clouded by rumor. But now, for the first time, there has been made public a remarkable document, the detailed directive that Joseph Petrosino was to follow in Sicily. This schedule of operations was discovered in the archives of the Department of Justice of the State of New York (Organized Crime and Racketeering Section). It also contains an explanatory introduction that probably came from Bingham himself. Here it is in its entirety:

Toward the end of last year, 1908, a program was presented to the Police Department of New York that, in the firm view of its author, an able criminologist thoroughly familiar with the methods of the

Italian underworld in this country and abroad, should prove effective in freeing New York of the many foreigners who have established a reign of lawlessness, extortion and murder here. This project was commissioned by Professor Jeremiah W. Jenks of Cornell University, and transmitted by him to the head of the Police Department of New York, Theodore Bingham. The man who drafted the proposal at Professor Jenk's request prefers not to be identified. He is an Italian expert who came to this country a few years ago and who addressed himself to immigration problems, with particular attention to that of crime. He is now employed in a special capacity by the United States Treasury.

The plan that he has evolved appears to us to be one of the most effective for weakening the strength of the "Black Hand" in this city. Since its key feature provides for the collection of evidence in Italy against men regarded here as dangerous, the plan calls for the appointment of secret agents in Italy and suggests that meanwhile a man be sent to Italy to recruit them. The plan itself was submitted to Professor Jenks by the expert already mentioned, with the following letter, dated 7 November 1908:

"Dear Professor Jenks:

"I have the pleasure of presenting for your consideration the report that you requested from me on Italian criminal activity in the United States, as well as some suggestions that, in my opinion, could lead to highly satisfactory results.

"In my statement I deal with only one specific form of criminality, quite different from the kind that usually arises out of ignorance of American laws or sudden bursts of passion. Those of whom I treat here are habitual criminals who were such in Italy and who, upon coming to America, have formed associations with others of the same kind and thus have come to constitute what is commonly called the 'Black Hand.' It is they, and they alone, who represent the decidedly undesirable element of Italian immigration.

"The ordinary Italian immigrant, as a rule, never becomes a criminal after his arrival in this country. If he is an honest man when he arrives in the United States for the first time, he remains one, for it is very difficult for him, given his habits and his very ignorance, to fall into that special cunning, intelligent form of local criminal class that exists in the United States. In my opinion, almost ninety per cent of the Italian criminals in the United States were already lawbreakers in Italy, and I am certain that proper investigations into their pasts would fully corroborate this.

"Italian criminals reach America in three different ways:

"1. As second- or third-class passengers, or in steerage, with passports obtained through political connections or bribery, inasmuch as it would be impossible for a criminal to obtain a passport from the Italian government otherwise.

"2. With passports issued to them under false names.

"3. By obtaining assistance in boarding ships clandestinely in Italian harbors, without passports, by persons who have made a business of this.

"Italian criminals who come to the United States can be separated into various classes:

"1. Italians who, having committed crimes in Italy and served time in prison, have come to America in order to avoid the consequent special surveillance.

"2. Italians who have committed crimes in Italy and fled here before trial.

"3. Italians who are universally regarded as criminals but against whom the public authorities have never succeeded in proving a specific crime. They take refuge here either because they are forced to flee by public opinion or because they fear possible incrimination or revenge by their enemies.

"To these three decidedly criminal classes must be added another, which I had the opportunity to discover when I worked for the United States Customs Service. This class is that of the smugglers: a category of men inured to risks, not habitual criminals in the ordinary sense of the word but in many instances previously sentenced for minor offenses in Italy, and prepared to ally themselves with real criminals when they get the chance.

"Such are the various types of Italian criminals who come to the United States; the reasons that lead them to leave Italy are as follows:

"*Special surveillance* is the nightmare of Italian offenders. It is a peculiar form of restriction of individual liberty invoked by Italian courts when, on the basis of the defendant's character and his bad record, it is believed that he will commit further crimes as soon as he is free.

"As this law is applied, the ex-convict must remain in his regular place of residence for a period of two to four years after his release;

report to the local police authorities two or three times per week; be in his home before six o'clock every evening. If he is picked up with weapons, or in a state of intoxication, or in suspicious places or company, or behaves suspiciously, he is sent back to prison (see Italian penal regulations of 18.x.1896).

"Now the primary reason why criminals come to America, a reason that it is very important to take into consideration here, is the ease with which it is possible to evade punishment in the United States. The following comparison may demonstrate the practical truth of this statement:

"In the United States, 10,662 persons were tried for homicide in 1896; in Italy the number was 3,606. The proportion, given the respective populations of the two countries, is almost the same. But, whereas in Italy sixty-two per cent of those tried were convicted, the percentage of verdicts of guilty in the United States was only 1.3. This clearly shows the reason for the continual increase in the immigration of Italian criminals to America.

"Here surveillance by the police is virtually non-existant. Here it is easy to get hold of weapons and explosives for criminal purposes. Here there is no penalty for giving a false name and address, whereas in Italy there is one. Here it is easy to hide, partly because of the vast size of the country, and partly because of the extreme density of population in the larger cities, along with the variability in laws and statutes from state to state. To all this, which makes police action long-drawn-out and often fruitless, must be added the ease with which freedom on bail may be obtained.

"Another factor to be taken into consideration is that, within a short time following their arrival in America, many of the most hardened Italian criminals become associated with certain political cliques for which they work and from which they receive unlimited protection in return. I have often heard people say, when a criminal has by some miracle escaped a verdict of guilty: 'There's no way to get at him. He belongs to Tammany (the central organization of the Democratic Party).'

"The notorious Paul and Jim Kelly, gang chiefs on the Lower East Side, are Italians associated with political clubs, and the immunity that they enjoy is confirmation of what I have said.

"As an Italian who has studied the various aspects of the criminal element in Italy, it is very easy for me to understand why these people look to the United States as the Promised Land. And in fact I could supply names and instances of Sicilian gangs that have sentenced someone to death and then, by threat or by ruse, prevailed on him to emigrate to America so that they could kill him here with greater ease and less danger of getting caught.

"But I have no need to cite such examples here. Every crime committed by a Sicilian in the past three years, the perpetrator of which the police have failed to identify, is proof of my contention.

"Although in theory it is very difficult for a criminal to get a passport in Italy, I have already explained that it is in fact feasible. And in addition, on the basis of unchallengable reports and documents, I could show how in the past month alone more than a hundred Italians have been smuggled into the United States without passports. Under these conditions, and until special regulations and special laws have been introduced, the best course is to examine how the situation may be dealt with under the existing law (that of July, 1907).

"Sections 2 and 19 of that law establish that any alien entering this country illegally may be expelled and deported to his country of origin provided that the arrest takes place within three years of the date of his arrival. Now this law, vigorously implemented, would be adequate to effect a drastic reduction in the ranks of the Italian underworld in the United States and would lead in a very short time to a decrease in crime by substantially curbing the influx of new criminals.

"I will not proceed to demonstrate how it would be possible to identify and expel any Italian who had a prior criminal record in his own country and whose entrance into the United States, with or without passport, was therefore accomplished in violation of the law.

"The document that gives the American authorities the right to order expulsion is the 'penal certificate,' which is issued by an Italian tribunal and attests to the fact that the person in question has one or more convictions for specific crimes or else the 'police certificate,' which describes him as a person of bad character even though he has never been specifically convicted of anything. Copies of these certificates can easily be obtained in Italy, since any lawyer can request them from the offices of the courts without having to state any reason.

"I myself have asked for and received a great number of these certificates for the Police Department of the City of New York. But in order to get them, of course, it is necessary to provide the court with the precise identification of the person in question, including the date and place of his birth and the names of his parents. Now it is obvious that it would be quite difficult to obtain these data from the criminal himself who, on the contrary, has every reason to falsify them in part or wholly in such a way as to throw off the search. Instead it would be necessary to proceed in the opposite direction, and to maintain agents in those Italian provinces in which crime is highest and from which most criminals leave for the United States. These agents, with the backing of the local authorities or through private sources, would have to ascertain where and under what names the criminal emigrants are living in the United States. Equipped then with the appropriate penal certificates, the American authorities would be able to initiate deportation proceedings.

"It is almost impossible to carry this out by mail, since it would be extremely difficult to try to clarify these matters and obtain the desired information by letter. The work that is required is of a difficult nature, and it is not certain whether, from here, one could recruit suitable persons to whom to give assignments with any assurance that they could carry them out without intimidation and without giving in to bribery.

"What I propose in this situation is the following:

"1. Send to Italy a trustworthy person who knows the local details of the underworld, the Italian criminal procedures, and the American immigration laws. In a relatively brief time this individual could lay the groundwork as follows:

"a. First of all, obtain from the Italian judicial archives a list of criminals who have completed their terms in Italian prisons within the past six years. I say *six years* because it is not likely that a former prisoner who has lived in Italy for more than six years after the termination of his sentence and police surveillance would then decide to come to America.

"b. Through the police or private sources, determine who among such persons have entered the United States legally or illegally. If possible, get their photographs and addresses, and thus be sure of obtaining the penal certificates required in order to launch deportation proceedings here.

"2. Through the courts themselves, obtain vital statistics and detailed descriptions of criminals who have been convicted and whose terms will expire during the next six years. Such information, kept in systematic files, could provide the immigration authorities with the means to prevent the entrance of further criminals to the United States.

"3. In every Italian city and regional subdivision, in every town where courts sit in the provinces above specified, find an honest man (a lawyer if possible) who can combine his normal activities with others useful to us, following the methods described above and receiving compensation to cover his expenses, etc.

"If this enterprise could be carried out in the strongholds of the Mafia in Sicily and of the Camorra in Naples, in the infamous anarchist zones between Florence and Bologna, and in certain limited criminal zones in the north, it would be easy to spot every Italian criminal currently resident in the United States. Such a preliminary program could be carried out in about six months, and, once it was under way, an office in New York with a team of four or five detectives could proceed to track down the criminals and to draft warrants for deportation orders.

"As far as this detective team itself is concerned, I believe that it would be wise to appoint at least two men from Italy, chosen from among the best of the Italian police officers on active duty who speak English fluently. I think it would be easy to persuade two such officers to ask for leaves of absence for one or two years in order to come to America and perform these functions. No special formalities would be required to obtain such permission.

"There are various officers of the Italian police who have spent many years of their lives in the south and who know almost all the criminals there. They are men accustomed to military discipline and, once in this country, they could organize a highly efficient arm.

"As for the confidential agent to be sent at once to Italy, the cost (calculated on the basis of a six-month mission) would be as follows:

"Round-trip ticket, New York/Italy	$ 250
"Travel within Italy	1,500
"Wages for stenographers, etc., @ $100 per month per person	—
"Hotel expenses	2,000
"Salary, @ $500 per month	3,000

"There would be no other expenses except payment to private informants. Police information is free.

"The agents hired in Italy could be paid the equivalent of $2 or $3 for each criminal identified.

"Thanks to such a system, the United States authorities would be able to operate as follows:

"a. In the cases of criminals resident in the United States for less than three years, the penal certificates recording convictions would be sufficient to guarantee their deportation.

"b. In the cases of criminals now being sought by the Italian authorities, the police certificates would be sufficient for their deportation.

"c. As for criminals who have entered the United States illegally, confirmation from Italian sources that they had left their country secretly would be sufficient to send them back there.

"In this brief summary I have found it difficult to elaborate on the many advantages of the system; none the less I am certain that, if a confidential agent of the Police Department is sent to Italy, a man who can set up a network of informants *in loco,* we shall see many developments that it is at present impossible to predict, but the result will be unquestionably gratifying."

9. From New York to Genoa

LIEUTENANT JOSEPH PETROSINO left New York on February 9, 1909. He was not at all in good spirits. His closest colleagues, including Sergeant Vachris, who went to see him off, were to say later that he was in the worst of moods. Chiefly he was irritated at having to be away from his wife and his adored baby daughter for a long period, but he had other problems too.

According to Bingham's instructions, Petrosino was supposed to give the Italian authorities the impression that he had been entrusted by his government with an investigation of a general character, where actually he was to set up a secret information network that would operate in direct contact with the American police and without the knowledge of the Italian law-enforcement agencies. In a word, it was to be an espionage operation that would hardly have pleased the Italians in the event that it had come to their attention.

1. Italian immigrants on their arrival in New York.

2. A street in Little Italy.

3. Patrolman
   Petrosino at
   the start of his
   career.

THE WORLD: THURSDAY EVENING, APRIL 23, 1903.

DETECTIVE PETROSINO AND SEVENTEEN DESPERATE CRIMINALS
WHOM HE HAS RUN DOWN, CONVICTED AND SENT TO PRISON.

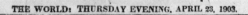

4. The story is summed up in the headline from *The*
   (New York) *World* for April 23, 1903.

5. Vito Cascio Ferro.

6. Carlo Costantino. 7. Antonino Passananti.

The X shows the place outside the fence that
surrounds the Garibaldi Garden in Piazza Marina
where Petrosino was killed.

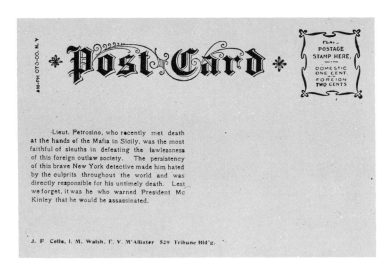

AM-PH OTO-CO. N. Y

✷ Post Card ✷

PLA-
POSTAGE
STAMP HERE.

DOMESTIC
ONE CENT.
FOREIGN
TWO CENTS

Lieut. Petrosino, who recently met death
at the hands of the Mafia in Sicily, was the most
faithful of sleuths in defeating the lawlessness
of this foreign outlaw society. The persistency
of this brave New York detective made him hated
by the culprits throughout the world and was
directly responsible for his untimely death. Lest
we forget, it was he who warned President Mc
Kinley that he would be assassinated.

J. F. Cella, J. M. Walsh, F. V. M'Allister 829 Tribune Bld'g.

9–10. A commemorative postcard sold in the United
States after the detective's death.

A Martyr To His Duty

Lieut. Joseph Petrosino, New York.
New York Police Department,
1869-1909
Assassinated in discharge of his duty,
At Palermo, Italy, March 12, 1909.

11. One of the last photographs of Petrosino.

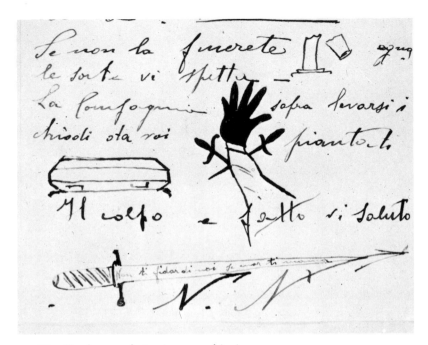

12. Detail of one of the innumerable letters sent to the authorities of Palermo by anonymous writers who claimed to have killed Petrosino.

13. Petrosino's gravestone in New York.
14. The author with Petrosino's daughter Adelina.

So the stakes were very high. If the attempt had succeeded, many interests would have suffered and the story of the Italian underworld in America today would probably be different. Petrosino was at the center of the gamble. He had the key that could have closed the gates of the United States to the immigration of Italian criminals virtually in his pocket. And obviously he could not have been unaware of the great personal danger that the undertaking entailed.

His departure from New York was cloaked in maximum secrecy. A few days earlier the rumor was deliberately spread through police circles that the lieutenant had suffered a relapse after his recent illness and that his doctor had ordered him to take a long rest. Only Bingham and his closest associates knew the truth.

Petrosino sailed on the liner *Duca di Genova,* bound directly for Genoa, under the assumed identity of Simone Velletri, a Jewish business man. He did not permit even his wife to accompany him to the pier. His luggage consisted of two big new yellow-leather suitcases. In his pocket he carried official letters of introduction addressed to the Italian Minister of the Interior and the head of Italy's police forces, Francesco Leonardi, as well as a notebook containing the names of a number of criminals (at the top of the list were Giuseppe Morello, Ignazio Lupo, Giuseppe Fontana, Carlo Costantino and Antonino Passananti). It was his intention to go personally to pick up their penal certificates in order to expedite the extradition proceedings already instituted by the American authorities. He also had a list of potential informers whom he intended to approach as soon as he reached Sicily. Inside one of his suitcases was his police revolver, a .38-caliber Smith & Wesson, with its regulation holster.

Traveling in first class, the detective was assigned Stateroom 10, which had three berths. The steward serving this stateroom was Giuseppe Izzo. Altogether there were one hundred ninety-two passengers aboard the ship; fifty-three were bound for Genoa, while the rest planned to transfer to another ship of the same line and go on to Naples or Palermo. There were only fourteen passengers in first class.

A few days before he sailed, Joseph Petrosino had completed

a complicated investigation of certain Sicilian criminals who specialized in forced prostitution. For some time they had been operating in conjunction with accomplices working in Sicily. Theirs was a simple system: from time to time these accomplices sent their American colleagues the names and addresses of local girls who had begun to be talked about or who for any reason wanted to leave the country. From the other end, the New York headquarters saw to it that the girls themselves, or their parents, were supplied with letters from "honest, hardworking young Sicilians who would like to have wives from their own country beside them in faraway America." This was followed by the usual exchanges of letters and photographs until the girls decided to accept the proposals of marriage and the free passage sent to them by their unknown suitors. The rest is easy to imagine. Once they had reached New York, the girls were met by very different people waiting for them at the dock. Through cajolery or through threats, they wound up as prostitutes.

Petrosino had succeeded in breaking up this gang and sending its leaders to prison. Only one of them had escaped conviction. He was Paolo Palazzotto, born twenty-seven years earlier in Palermo. Even so, the young man had not come out safe; he had been arrested again by Joseph Corrao of the Italian Squad and turned over to Petrosino, by whom he had been badly beaten before he was moved to Ellis Island for deportation to Italy.

Palazzotto was to have been sent out on the same ship, the *Duca di Genova,* on which Petrosino sailed. His departure had been postponed, however, because he had had to be hospitalized (it would appear that the cause was the loss of teeth that the detective lieutenant had knocked out by punching him with a fist filled with keys). But there were other "undesirables" aboard for whose expulsion Petrosino was responsible. Two of these were Leonardo Crimi and Domenico Saidone.

The *Duca di Genova* sailed at four o'clock in the afternoon. In spite of the piercing cold, Joseph Petrosino stayed on deck a long time, watching the city vanish into the mist. To say that he had ominous premonitions would be unwarranted fantasy; but the fact remains that he was very somber. This was to be confirmed subsequently by the ship's captain, Giovanni Orengo, and some of the lieutenant's fellow passengers. In addition, he became seasick immediately and had to spend a few days in his cabin under the care of Izzo, the steward, who brought him "solid food."

Petrosino soon recovered, and he struck up an acquaintance with one Francesco Delli Bovi, thirty years old, who, it turned out, lived in Muro Lucano. They were so frequently seen together that the theory was later offered that Delli Bovi was also a secret agent. Actually, this individual vanished immediately after his arrival in Genoa. No trace of him was ever found.

One evening the self-styled Simone Velletri was chatting with the ship's purser, Carlo Longobardi. "I know who you are," the purser said to him at one point. "I've seen your picture in the papers. But you can rely on my discretion."

According to what Longobardi subsequently testified, the detective seemed highly flattered at having been recognized. And, although he insisted that the purser say nothing to anyone, Petrosino did confide to him that he had "an important job to do in Italy." Thereupon the detective allowed himself the pleasure of talking about some of his more interesting cases.

Having grown accustomed to being pointed out in the street, Petrosino probably felt a certain irritation at playing the part of an ordinary traveler. There is no evidence, however, that he disclosed his real identity to anyone other than Longobardi and, perhaps, Delli Bovi. He became acquainted with other passengers and grew fond of Guglielmo Andreacci, a boy of twelve who was traveling with his mother, Rosa Florio of Bari. At one point he even let slip that he had known the boy's father, Domenico, who was employed as an interpreter in the Ellis Island reception center. On the other hand, the lieutenant did not explain the circumstances in which he had known the interpreter. With the other people he met aboard, such as Francesco Galli, a merchant from Lucca, in Tuscany, who was traveling with his wife and their son, Petrosino maintained his assumed identity. He told Galli that he was going to Italy to seek treatment for an intestinal infection, and Galli advised him to consult a Professor Cardarelli in Rome. It is curious to note that, even though his ticket had been issued in the name of Simone Velletri, Petrosino introduced himself to some of his traveling companions as Guglielmo Simone.

There was another amusing bit of gossip. One evening, at dinner, Petrosino mentioned to Galli that he planned to go to Palermo. "Be careful not to look at the women," Galli warned him jokingly. "Otherwise they'll kill you down there."

"I'm not afraid of anybody," Petrosino retorted sharply.

There was also a minor bit of melodrama during the voyage, and of course Petrosino had his part in it. In third class there was a passenger called Paolo Grattucci, who was consistently very insolent and very arrogant. Somehow he had been allowed to move freely in both the other classes; he took his meals in the second-class dining room and was served earlier and better than the other passengers. Perhaps he was merely a friend or a relative of someone in the crew; but there might also have been something else.

Grattucci's behavior came to light when a Roman engineer traveling in second class, twenty-eight-year-old Luigi Galassi, protested against the privileged treatment that the intruder was receiving. Grattucci immediately took offense and a lively quarrel followed. Then the two men encountered each other privately on deck and, after this meeting, Galassi went to the captain and requested protection claiming to be in fear of his life.

When Petrosino heard of this incident, he insisted on taking a personal hand in it. He went in search of Grattucci, exchanged a few quick remarks with him, and from then on Grattucci was never again seen where he did not belong.

The *Duca di Genova* docked in Genoa at six o'clock in the morning on February 21; she was about twenty-six hours late. Before he went ashore, Petrosino asked the purser, Longobardi, for the names of good hotels in Rome, Naples and Palermo. Longobardi suggested the Inghilterra in Rome, the Hôtel de Londras in Naples, and the Hôtel de France in Palermo.

After he had made his farewells to his fellow passengers, Petrosino left the ship alone, refusing to allow the porters to carry his baggage. From the harbor he took a carriage to the Principe railway station, where he boarded the first train for Rome. He did not waste a single minute in looking at Genoa.

His complicated mission had begun. He was now a man alone, who had been assigned a mission unquestionably too big for any one person, and he rolled up his sleeves and prepared to meet a powerful but invisible enemy. If the purpose of his mission to Sicily had been made known, he would automatically have become a walking target. But Petrosino was confident that he was protected by secrecy. And, as he set foot in Italy, he renewed the promise that he had made to himself as he left New York: to trust no one. In his mind he could still hear the last thing that the loyal Vachris had said to him: "Watch out, boss. Down there everything's Mafia."

As the policeman was traveling toward Rome, convinced that his mission was being carried out in secrecy, millions of Americans had known the purposes of his journey for more than twenty-four hours. The disconcerting revelation had been made by the *New York Herald* of February 20 and, what is even more unbelievable, the source of its story was the Police Commissioner himself, Theodore Bingham. This is what the *Herald* said:

As the first step in the work of the new Secret Service established by Commissioner Bingham, Lieutenant Joseph Petrosino has gone to Italy, specifically to Sicily, in order to obtain important information bearing on Italian criminals residing in the United States and in particular in New York, where the police, who would like to initiate the deportation of many criminals, lack the necessary evidence of their records in Italy.

In addition, many of them have been tried and convicted in Italy *in absentia* and are wanted by the police of that country. Thus their identification will be sufficient to allow proceedings for their extradition. In this way the Secret Service will succeed in ridding the city of many dangerous individuals against whom it has not previously been possible to file specific charges.

Why did Bingham release so sensitive a story to the press? Probably to get publicity for himself. It was a period of political campaigning, and perhaps the ambitious Commissioner was incapable of holding out against the temptation to make an impression on the voters. We can rule out the suspicion, which was later bruited about, that the leak of the story about Petrosino's secret mission was part of the conspiracy that was to cost the celebrated detective his life. To inform the leaders of the Black Hand it was hardly necessary to print the story in a newspaper.

The indiscretion, in any event, was repeated by every newspaper in New York. The story appeared also in the European edition of the *New York Herald,* published in Paris.

Now everyone knew of Petrosino's "secret" assignment. Anyone who had reason to fear his arrival in Sicily was now on notice.

In the meantime, two old acquaintances of the detective had gone back to Partinico unexpectedly. They were Carlo Costantino, alias Giovanni Pecoraro, alias Tommaso Petto, and Antonino Passananti, two notorious members of the "Black Hand" in New York and both implicated at the time in the famous "barrel murder."

They had arrived in Naples on February 17 aboard the liner *Romanic,* which had sailed from New York at almost the same time as the *Duca di Genova.* Even though they had no unfinished business with the Italian authorities, they had traveled under false names and papers. Costantino had turned into Vincenzo Carbone, Passananti into Antonino D'Amico.

Their return to Partinico was a surprise to everyone. Even their friends and families had not been forewarned. In fact, a short time earlier Costantino had written to his parents that he had built a fine house in Brooklyn, where he intended to take up residence with his wife.

Both men were very different now from the two penniless youths who had sailed for America six years before. Now they were unquestionably rich; they brought masses of gifts for their relatives, and Costantino deposited thirty thousand lire in the Back of Sicily, though the account was opened in the name of his brother-in-law, Salvatore Inghilleri.

The day after his arrival, Costantino sent a cable from Partinico to New York. The telegraph operator in the post office found it so strange that he felt obliged to send a copy of it to the local chief of public safety, Cavalier Augusto Battioni. It said: "I Lo Baido work Fontana." It was addressed to "Giuseppe Morello, New York, 360 East 61 Street." Apparently this was a code message that only the head of the Black Hand in America would be able to understand.

After a few days with their families, Costantino and Passananti went to Bisaquino for a visit to their old friend Vito Cascio Ferro.

10. Rome–Naples–Palermo

THE PARIS-ROME EXPRESS, which Petrosino had boarded in Genoa, arrived at the Italian capital in the evening. The policeman, who had traveled alone in a first-class compartment, came out of the station with his big suitcases and entered a carriage. "Take me to the Hotel Inghilterra," he told the driver in his heavy accent.

At the hotel, in Via Bocca di Leone, Petrosino registered under the name of Guglielmo Simone and was given Room 9. He shut himself up in it at once, refusing dinner. He was tired and worn from the strain of his long journey.

The next day, February 22, he went out at about ten in the morning and asked to be taken to the United States Embassy. Even though it was a holiday, Petrosino was astonished at the festive atmosphere that filled the streets. He asked his driver the reason.

"Today is Shrove Tuesday," the driver explained. "Carnival."

Even the embassy was closed. "Are you people celebrating the carnival too?" he asked the doorkeeper.

"No, sir. The embassy is closed because today is George Washington's birthday."

Petrosino took advantage of the unexpected rest to make a quick tour of the center of Rome. Later he went back to the hotel and, in his shaky Italian, wrote a letter to his brother, Vincenzo, who had gone back some years earlier to live in the family's old house in Padula.

Rome, 22 February 1909

Dear brother,

I imagine you'll be surprised when you hear I'm in Rome on a secret job. Don't let anybody know but in a short time I'm coming to see you. When I come I'll let you know by telegram. Again I repeat not to let anybody know anything, not even your wife.

I greet you with affection.

Your brother,
Giuseppe

P.S. I came to Rome yesterday.

In the afternoon Petrosino went out again. He strolled along Via Sistina and then headed for Piazza San Silvestro, passing in front of the Press Club. A number of newspaper men were in the club and two of them immediately recognized the policeman. One was Camillo Cianfarra, editor of *l'Araldo* in New York (the Italian-language daily connected with the *New York Herald*), who had been sent to Italy on special assignment to report the recent earthquake in Messina; the other was Guido Memmo, the same paper's regular Rome correspondent.

The correspondents ran out to greet Petrosino. "Joe! What the devil are you doing in Rome?" Cianfarra asked. This time Petrosino did not disguise the fact that he was irritated at having been recognized.

"Quiet, please," he whispered. "Don't say my name. You'll ruin me!"

"All right, all right," Cianfarra said. "But what are you doing here?"

"Perhaps Giolitti really sent for you to handle the elections for him?" Memmo suggested with a smile. At the moment an Italian political campaign was indeed at its height. The elections were to be held on February 28.

"Not exactly," Petrosino smiled back. "But in any case, if you care about my friendship, do me the favor of not telling anybody you saw me. I'm here on business, of course. But I have a couple of days to myself, and I really need somebody to play guide and show me this beautiful city."

In a few minutes the three men were riding in a carriage. Thus Petrosino had the opportunity to see all the monuments of Rome, and he was deeply impressed by them. To his two friends he acknowledged his intention of going to Sicily to carry out some investigations; but at the same time he implied that the chief reason for his trip was a case of counterfeit American currency that had been uncovered in Milan.

During the sightseeing, Petrosino noticed that he was being followed by a stranger. Seeing that he had been discovered, the man fled precipitately, but the policeman and the two correspondents turned the tables and followed him. After a long walk, they saw the man heading for the telegraph window in the post office in Piazza San Silvestro; there he sent a telegram.

"I've seen that man before," Petrosino told his friends, "but I don't remember where." Later they managed to learn that the unknown man had sent his telegram to Noto, Sicily, but they had no opportunity of reading it. Cianfarra himself told of the incident in a story in *l'Araldo.*

In the evening the three friends dined in a private room in the Umberto I Restaurant in Via della Mercede; the waiter who served them was named Federico Antonelli. As they were leaving afterward, Petrosino once more heard someone address him by name. It was the former Consul General in New York, Carlo Branchi, who was dining with friends. He and Petrosino greeted each other warmly and made an appointment for the following day. Petrosino also promised the two reporters that he would see them the next day, but neither they nor Branchi ever saw him again after that evening.

On February 23 Petrosino called on the United States Ambassador, Lloyd A. Griscom, who told him that he had already received instructions from Washington and that he would at once take the steps necessary to arrange for the detective to see the Italian Minister of the Interior and the head of the police.

Back in his hotel room, Petrosino wrote a long letter in Italian to his wife:

Rome, 23 February 1909

My dearest wife,

I sent you a cable that I was in the Eternal City. The people of Rome are celebrating carnival and all the public offices are closed, so I haven't been able to see the officials I wanted to see, and I won't be able to before tomorrow. Therefore I have to stay here a few days longer, and then I'll go to Sicily. From there I'll let you know where in the island, but I think I'll go to Palermo.

I've seen St. Peter's, the Sistine Chapel, and Michelangelo's Galleries, which are the wonders of the world. At the sight of St. Peter's I was spellbound. It is beyond human imagination. What a huge, magnificent place! The church could easily hold a hundred-and-fifty-thousand people. But how can I give you any idea of it? These are things you have to see with your own eyes. No description can possibly give you an idea of it. I don't think there's anything greater in the whole world.

I saw the Italian Parliament, the Senate, and the Ministry of Justice. I also saw the palace where the Queen Mother lives, and the great historic buildings of ancient Rome. They must go back three thousand years, but they are still marvelous. To see everything properly you would have to stay in Rome for years.

In spite of everything I am sad, and I must say that, when it comes to comfort, I prefer dear old New York, which I hope to see again very soon. I hope too that my partner won't take much longer to get here, because I'm tired of being all alone here.*

In any case it seems as if it's a thousand years before I go home. Here the people are totally different, also often the police don't give you any help when you ask them questions. Food costs just

---

*Petrosino was probably referring to the man who was supposed to take his place once his mission had been completed. The New York Police Department, however, has always denied that there was any such plan. As a result, the reference to an early arrival is inexplicable.—Author.

as much here as in New York but people earn much less. We had a stormy trip from New York to Genoa. The ship docked twenty-six hours late. All the passengers were sick, some more than others. Nobody managed to eat anything except me—I had a good appetite all through the voyage and never felt the ocean at all.

Kiss my dear little girl for me and remember me to all our friends and relatives. A kiss from your affectionate husband,

Giuseppe Petrosino

On the morning of February 24 Petrosino was introduced to Giolitti's principal private secretary, Camillo Peano, by the United States Ambassador. Their talk was short and formal. The policeman briefly explained the purposes of his "study trip" and Peano (whom Petrosino took to be the Minister of the Interior) took leave of him with the suggestion that he communicate directly with the head of the police, Francesco Leonardi.

Petrosino, without an escort, went to see Leonardi the following day. "My name is Petrosino," he said as he entered.

Leonardi was somewhat taken aback. "To tell the truth," he admitted later, "I did know his name. But I had the impression that he thought of himself as being far more famous than he actually was."

The two policemen talked for about a half-hour. Petrosino presented a letter of introduction written by Bingham and then explained the official reasons for his journey without, of course, giving even the slightest hint of his plan for setting up a private information network.

Before they took leave of each other, Leonardi gave Petrosino a letter addressed to all police commissioners in Sicily. It said:

> Signor Giuseppe Petrosino, a Lieutenant in the Police of New York, is traveling to Sicily on instructions from the Government of the United States in order to conduct investigations and research having to do with the study of the various manifestations of crime in international relations. Your Honors are therefore urged to afford all possible facilities to Signor Giuseppe Petrosino in order to complete the mission entrusted to him.
>
> The Head of the Police
> Francesco Leonardi

On the morning of February 26 the detective sent his first report to Commissioner Bingham in the form of a letter:

Dear Commissioner Bingham:

I arrived at Rome at 8:20 P.M. on the 21st but this being the eve of the anniversary of Washington's birth and at the same time the start of the Roman carnival, which lasted two days, I was not able to see any of the persons whom I was supposed to see. Finally, through the good offices of the American Ambassador, I was able to meet the Minister of the Interior, the Honorable Mr. Peano, with whom I had a discussion on the subject of Italian criminals and their activities in the U.S.A. He was so much interested in this matter that he gave instructions to the Head of the Police, His Excellency Francesco Leonardi, to issue definitive orders to the Prefects, Sub-Prefects and Mayors of the entire kingdom not to issue passports to Italian criminals heading for the U.S.A. He also gave me a letter addressed to all the police commissioners in Sicily, Calabria and Naples with instructions to assist me in every way in the performance of my mission. Both the Minister and the Head of the Police had already heard of me. I also showed them the gold watch presented to me by the Italian Chief, which you know about.

Dear General, the trip was very rough: the weather was bad almost all the time. The ship was twenty-six hours late and I don't feel very well, and so, before I get right down to work, I will take a couple of days' rest. When I get to Palermo to start the "job," I will keep you continually informed of the results.

Wishing you and Mr. Woods* a long and happy life, I remain

Your very devoted
Joseph Petrosino

The American detective left Rome the next morning. His bill at the Inghilterra was thirty lire: six lire a night. Before he left the city, he sent a telegram to his brother, Vincenzo, saying that he would arrive at Padula by train at one-fifty-three in the afternoon.

A few hours later Petrosino was back in his native town. His brother, accompanied by a stranger, was waiting for him at the station.

*The Deputy Commissioner.—Author.

"Why didn't you come alone?" the detective asked his brother after they had embraced. He seemed quite irritated by the third person's presence.

"But this is our cousin, Vincenzo Arato, the son of our sainted mother's sister!" Vincenzo Petrosino explained.

This information seemed to calm the detective. "You know," he said, "my trip is secret. Nobody's supposed to know."

"That's exactly what I wanted to talk to you about," his brother said, taking a newspaper called *Il Pungolo* (*The Goad*) from his pocket. "Look." He pointed to a headline underlined in pencil. "Here it tells about your trip to Italy."

Angrily the detective snatched the paper from his brother's hand and read the story about him, reprinted from the *New York Herald*. Vincenzo heard him curse under his breath.

Joseph Petrosino stayed in Padula only a few hours. He did not want to see anyone, even though many people had gathered in front of the house to hail their celebrated fellow townsman. He did not want to visit the village in which he had been born. He stayed sulking inside his brother's house, barely speaking to him. Obviously he was very angry at what he had read in the newspaper; nonetheless he did not consider it necessary to alter his plans.

At seven in the evening he was again on a train, bound for Naples. Even to his brother he would not disclose his destination. "Maybe I'll go to Messina," he said. "On the way back I'll stop and see you again."

On the train he ate a frugal meal that had been prepared for him by his sister-in-law. As far as Naples he shared his compartment with Cavalier Valentino di Montesano, a former captain of Carabinieri who recognized him but pretended to the contrary.

11. Piazza Marina and Environs

PIAZZA MARINA IN PALERMO has lost much of its old magnificence. Its ancient palaces, with their great carriage gates that lead to inner courtyards and from there into networks of alleys that open to the rear, are crumbling, sinking to the level of furnished flats, on the verge of falling before the bulldozer. For years its two churches have been closed and slowly falling to pieces: San Giovannuzzo, at the corner of Corso Vittorio Emanuele, and San Giuseppe dei Miracoli, opposite at the corner of Via Longarini. The only thing that has remained intact is the Garibaldi Garden, a rectangular little jungle surrounded by a high grille fence and filled with splendid exotic plants.

There was a time when this square was a nerve center of the city. Situated close to the old harbor, at the extreme edge of the Arab quarter called the Kalsa, it was the seat of the Court of the

Holy Inquisition during Spanish rule, and as well the preferred place of execution for the victims.

At the beginning of the twentieth century Piazza Marina was the commercial center of Palermo precisely because of its proximity to the port. At night few people went there, partly because of the poor lighting, partly because of the shadows cast by the gardens in the center; but during the day it was extremely busy. On the northern side, which faced Palazzo Partanna, which has since been demolished, there was the terminus of the electric streetcars owned and operated by the Shukert firm; on the right-hand side, toward Via Porto Salvo, there was the well known Cafè (and restaurant) Oreto. Then came the offices of the Società di Navigazione Generale—the General Shipping Company; while on the side nearer the sea, alongside Palazzo Chiaramonte, just where the Inquisition's tribunal stood (today it is the customs headquarters), was one of the most elegant hotels in the city, the Hôtel de France, to which one came by way of a broad stairway that is still in existence today.

Joseph Petrosino saw this square for the first time on the morning of February 28, 1909; he had come by carriage from the nearby harbor where he had arrived at eight o'clock aboard the mail boat from Naples. The first thing that attracted his attention, however, was not the splendid garden but a row of posters on the building walls, calling on the voters of the First District of Palermo to elect Raffaele Palizzolo, "the friend of the People."

The first balloting was in fact to take place on the following day. Since the single-member constituency was then the rule, the second (runoff) balloting would be held on the following Sunday among the candidates who had not won absolute majorities in their respective districts.

Palizzolo had had to run in the First District of Palermo because he had been frustrated in his hope of representing the district of Caccamo, left vacant as a result of the death of the Marquis di Rudinì. Vittorio Emanuele Orlando, whose district it was at the time, had relinquished it and chosen instead that of Partinico. In consequence, Palizzolo, who was running as a monarchist, had now to reckon with a formidable opponent, the same Di Stefano, now a follower of Giolitti, who years earlier, after the embarrassing trial in Florence, had resigned in order to return the former convict to his seat in the Chamber. Obviously the stock of the "king of the Mafia" had suffered a major slump.

The candidates in the two other districts in Palermo were Empedocle Restivo, Giovanni Pecoraro, and Pietro di Trabia; Vito Cascio Ferro's protege, the Honorable Domenico De Michele Ferrantelli, was running in the district of Bivona against a radical lawyer named Imbornone and a Socialist railway worker, Umberto Bianchi.

Petrosino went directly to the Hôtel de France and took Room 16 (five lire per night), registering under another false name— Simone Valenti di Giudea.

A few hours later he was in the office of the American consul in Palermo, William A. Bishop, in Palazzo Pecoraino, which was in Piazza Castelnuovo. He told the consul of his plans and indicated his intention of getting down to work at once. He also told the consul that he had informants in Palermo who would collaborate with him. When he left the consulate he went to the Banca Commerciale and opened an account in his own name with a deposit of two thousand lire. He also asked the manager's permission to have his mail addressed in care of the bank. This request was approved and the manager (who had had a prior consultation with Bishop) promised to observe the utmost secrecy as to the activities of his strange customer.

In the afternoon, accompanied by someone who has never been identified, the detective went to the courthouse, specifically to the department of penal certificates, to look into the records of certain individuals whose names appeared on his list. No one asked him for any explanations and he was left to work freely for several hours. Leaving the courthouse, he took a carriage to the office of a firm called A. Capra, where he rented a Remington typewriter for a month. He left a deposit of ten lire and signed the receipt in the name of Salvatore Basilicò.

At eight-thirty in the evening he dined quickly in the Cafè Oreto, sitting alone at a corner table. He left at nine-fifteen, turned left and took the shortest route back to the Hôtel de France, which was on the opposite side of the square. He was tired, nervous and irritated. As soon as he was in his room he wrote another letter—which was to be his last—to his wife. From its text it is easy to see what was his state of mind:

Weinen's Hôtel de France

Palermo, 28 February 1909

My dearest wife,

I have arrived in Palermo I am completely confused and it seems a thousand years till I come home. I don't like anything about Italy at all which I'll explain it to you when I come home. God, God, what misery! I was sick for five days. It was influenza and I had to stay in Rome, but now I feel all right. So send all messages to the Banca Commerciale di Palermo which is my address.

Say hello to Angelina and Luigi. Kiss Cousin Arturo for me and also my brother, Antonio, and his family, my friend, Carlucci, and his family. Greet your sister and her husband, to my dear Baby and to you thousands and thousands of kisses.

Your most aff. brother [sic]
Joseph Petrosino

The next day, Sunday, Petrosino spent in the hotel, making typewritten copies of the penal certificates that he had examined in the court offices. Then he put them into an envelope with a covering letter addressed to Commissioner Bingham:

Palermo, 1 March 1909

Hon. Theodore A. Bingham
Police Commissioner
Dear Sir:

Following my cablegram, I enclose the penal certificates of Gioacchino Candela and others. I have been in bed with influenza for the past week and just today I received your cablegram, because I could not go to Palermo before the 28th ult. Now I feel a little better and I am getting to work. I will explain everything to you in full in my next letter. There is nothing in the penal

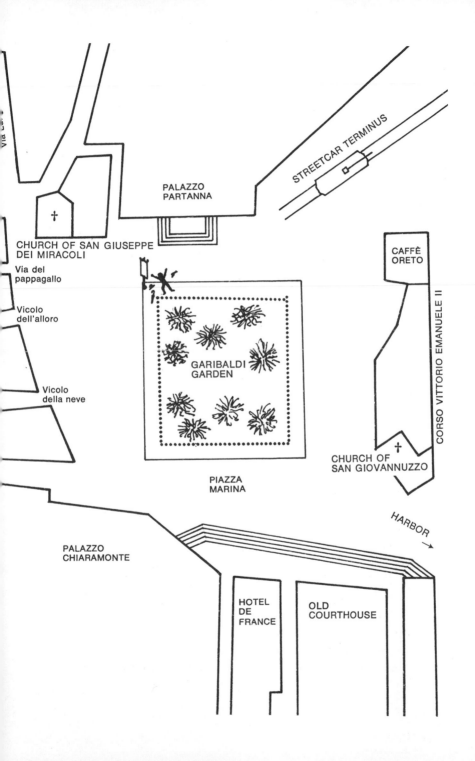

files dealing with Manatteri, Pericò and Matranga. Maybe I will find something about them later.

Faithfully,
Joseph Petrosino
P.S.: Send all mail to Banca Commerciale, Palermo, Italy.

From February 28 until March 6 Joseph Petrosino made a point of avoiding any contact with the Italian police. He roamed through Palermo and nearby towns, using a different name every so often, frequently disguising himself as well, and without leaving any trace of his presence. Unquestionably he talked with many people; he had told his men in New York that as soon as he reached Sicily he would make use of some of his old informants from Little Italy who had since gone back home. The fact that none of them was heard from after the murder of the detective should surprise no one. If indeed they were genuine informants, they would obviously be afraid of the inevitable vengeance of the Mafia. If, on the other hand, as is much more likely, they were decoys who had been instructed to lure Petrosino into the lethal trap, their silence is even more understandable.

It was not until March 5, then, that Petrosino informed Bishop, the consul, whom he went to see every day, that he planned to call on the city's Police Commissioner. "I don't trust the Italian police at all," he said. "I've learned things here that would make your hair stand on end."

Bishop agreed with a smile. "You can't tell me anything about them. I know a little too, after living here for five years! Nevertheless," he continued, "under the new Commissioner things have changed a bit. He was sent down from Milan specifically to clean the Mafia elements out of the police administration."

"I'll go and see him tomorrow," Petrosino said. "You'll have to introduce me."

Commissioner Baldassare Ceola had been transferred to Palermo on July 15, 1907. In Milan, where he had worked for ten years, he had had to concern himself indirectly with a tragic but sensational affair: on July 29, 1900, an anarchist from America had assassinated King Umberto I of Italy. Now, nine years later, a policeman, also from America, was inadvertently about to involve him in a no-less-sensational business.

At eleven o'clock in the morning of March 6, when he was informed that a stranger was waiting to see him and had an introduction from the American consul, Commissioner Ceola was in a good humor. The first day's vote had turned out favorably for the government's candidates and the next Sunday's ballots would surely confirm this first success. Giovanni Giolitti, who was both Premier and Minister of the Interior, would certainly congratulate him.

In a few minutes Petrosino was in the private office. As soon as he had read Bishop's letter of introduction and the other from Leonardi, the head of the police, Ceola greeted the visitor with great cordiality. "I've heard a great deal about you," he said. "What can I do to help you?"

"I have been instructed by my government to find out whether the passports issued to Italian emigrants conform to the laws," Petrosino explained. "Too many criminals are getting into my country from Sicily. We're tired of it."

Ceola recognized the reproach implicit in the reply. "The passports issued by this office are always completely legal," he said coldly.

"Then why is it that many of the criminals I have arrested showed perfectly clean penal certificates even though they had been convicted here?"

"Perhaps because they had been rehabilitated," Ceola pointed out. "You know what the procedure of rehabilitation is, I suppose?"

"No, I don't know anything about that. All I know is that you people send us gangsters with absolutely clean records. It's just this strange way of doing things that my government intends to get rid of."

"I saw at once," Ceola was to write later to the Prefect, "that Lieutenant Petrosino, to his disadvantage, was not a man of excessive education. Among other things, he was ignorant of our rules, and so I explained to him what the system of rehabilitation was . . .'"

But, of course, he did not explain to Petrosino that it was the general custom to "rehabilitate" criminals and Mafiosi just when they asked for passports to go to America.

From the very start of the conversation Petrosino felt hostility and aversion to this elegant official who treated him with a certain air of paternal condescension. And his suspicions of the Italian police were intensified.

"In any event," Commissioner Ceola was now saying, "consider me at your disposal. In fact, I'll make arrangements at once for you to have a bodyguard."

Petrosino shook his head vigorously. "Thank you, but I don't want a bodyguard."

"But it will be dangerous for you to wander alone round Palermo!" Ceola exclaimed. "You're too well known. The newspapers have announced your arrival in Italy, and no one knows how many enemies you have in this city."

"I also have friends in Palermo, Commissioner," Petrosino retorted with huffy dignity. "They will be enough to protect me."

"I envy you your confidence, Lieutenant," Ceola cut him short; the American's evident distrust was beginning to irritate him. "May I know, at any rate, where you are staying?"

"I have no intention of revealing that," Petrosino replied. "You can get in touch with me through my country's consulate."

At this point Ceola rang for a clerk and told him to ask Cavalier Poli, the commander of the Mobile Brigade, to come to his office at once. "Cavalier Poli," Ceola explained to Petrosino when the official arrived, "is a first-class officer. You can turn to him in matters of any kind at all. And now, if you will excuse me, I must get back to work." The Police Commissioner was clearly annoyed.

Petrosino and Poli went into another room to talk. But Petrosino did not wish to reveal his address to Poli either. "I will come to see you when I need to consult you," he said. Whereupon he left.

Subsequently Poli went to report to his superior. "I have the feeling that he has absolutely no confidence in us," he said of Petrosino. "All I could get from him was the promise that he would not leave Palermo without letting me know."

Ceola shrugged. "Let him do things his way; but don't let him get too far away."

In the next few days Petrosino had several meetings with Poli, arranging them by letter; but he refused to go back again to Police Headquarters. Their meetings were, in essence, technical, and they did not result in even the slightest personal relationship. Petrosino gave Poli summaries of the inquiries that he had made and asked for further information concerning offenders in whom he was interested.

Cavalier Poli saw at once that his American colleague must indeed have a certain number of informers at his disposal, and that some of these must be persons in high places. In fact, certain sensitive information in Petrosino's possession could have been acquired only by persons who had legitimate access to judicial circles. Poli also told Ceola that he was beginning to fear for Petrosino's safety, since the detective had proved to be rash enough to venture alone, even at night, into the very worst quarters of Palermo, where he held mysterious conferences with unidentified persons.

"Lieutenant Petrosino," Ceola was to write later in his report to Giolitti, "visited the most dangerous underworld areas; established relations, even where there was no need to do so, with persons in public office; talked too much, often, and readily even with the employees of the Cafè Oreto where he took his meals; carried a large part of his correspondence and his notes in his pockets. In short, while he manifested a reticence carried to the extreme toward the Questura [Police Headquarters] and his own consul, in all his dealings with everyone else he never exercised that elementary prudence that was absolutely essential not only for the preservation of his own life but as well for the success of the delicate mission that he had assumed. In every way he adhered to the custom of those among the Sicilians who believe that they get the best protection when, instead of turning to the Authorities and the forces of Law and Order, they put their trust in some notorious and dreaded criminal who has authority and influence in the underworld."

Even though Baldassare Ceola was obviously exaggerating, there is, in this passage, the whole picture of Petrosino with his courage, his vigor, and, above all, his natural exhibitionism. And there is no question that he was troubling the surrounding waters much too much and sowing alarm in Palermo's criminal circles.

"What the hell does this cop want?" many Mafiosi must have wondered. "Is he trying to keep Sicilians from going to America and making a living? Or is he trying to make trouble for people who've come back from America to enjoy their loot?" Surely questions like this must have gone the rounds of the Palermo gangsters, none of whom, certainly, had any reason to rejoice at Petrosino's arrival. Some like Vito Cascio Ferro, Costantino, and Passananti had prosecution hanging over them in the United States; others had friends or relatives in America who were now threatened with deportation; still others were afraid that now a barrier was going to block the only way to safety whenever it might be necessary to flee the island. Even if, as appears to have been the case, the conspiracy against the detective was planned in America, it had in Palermo a most fertile soil in which to take root and grow.

Ignorant of—or, rather, indifferent to—the dangers that were gathering round him, Joseph Petrosino continued his work. He was so confident of being protected that very often he went out unarmed. Apparently his mysterious informants had succeeded in winning the suspicious American policeman's complete confidence.

On March 11 Petrosino went to see Bishop again. He talked to the consul about his work and informed him that the next morning he was going to Caltanissetta to carry out further investigations in the courthouse there.

"Please don't say anything about this to anybody," he added. "I promised the Italian police not to leave Palermo without telling them first, but I have absolutely no intention of keeping my promise. Besides, I'll be back the same day. I have an appointment here in Palermo at four o'clock in the afternoon, and another one, very important, about nine in the evening."

When he left the consulate, Piazza Castelnuovo was crowded with would-be emigrants, waiting as usual outside the consulate for the visas that would get them out of Sicily. This morning, however, the crowd included an old acquaintance of the detective—

that Paolo Palazzotto whom he had had deported from America a few weeks before. Palazzotto had arrived in Naples aboard the liner *Indiano* on March 2. Turned over to the Carabinieri, he had been sent to Palermo, but there he had been set free immediately. Now he was outside the consulate with his friend, Ernesto Militano, a young man celebrated as the owner of "the finest pair of moustaches in Palermo." But Militano was known to the police for other reasons as well. The police authorities in his locality described him: "Militano is an incorrigible robber of prostitutes. Every night he makes the tour of the city's brothels, choosing a woman in each, going to bed with her, and then, after the act, not only refusing to pay her her legitimate fee but also robbing her of her night's earnings."

Petrosino walked past both men without noticing them and got into the carriage that was waiting for him. Palazzotto, however, as soon as he saw the detective, made an angry movement and set off to follow him, but Militano dissuaded him. Then, speaking in a loud voice so that everyone could hear, and pointing to the carriage as it moved off, Palazzotto said: "There goes Petrosino, the enemy of the Sicilians. He's come to Palermo to get himself killed!"

The detective, of course, had not heard him. He went to the Banca Commerciale, where he withdrew two hundred lire from his account. Of the two thousand deposited on February 28 he had now withdrawn one thousand two hundred, a substantial part. Probably he had used the money to pay his informants.

That evening there was another episode worth recalling. As Petrosino was having dinner, according to his custom, in the Cafè Oreto, Paolo Palazzotto and Ernesto Militano came in and went to the bar, where they stood drinking wine. They were noticed looking threateningly at the detective, who was eating alone. In a few minutes two other criminals came in—Francesco Nono and Salvatore Seminara. Seminara had been deported from the United States months earlier, again through Petrosino's intervention.

These two also spent some time at the bar, every now and then eying the detective and muttering to each other. A customer named Volpe, who was a police agent, was sitting nearby, listening, and he later reported this curious dialogue in dialect:

NONO (laughing): "But you know parsley [petrosino] gives you diarrhea!"

SEMINARA (threateningly): "If I die, they'll bury me, but, if I get over it, I'll kill him!"

NONO: "You haven't got the guts."

SEMINARA: "You don't know the Seminaras."

A little after nine o'clock Petrosino left the restaurant and went back to his hotel. It was cold, and a storm was gathering.

The next morning he rose early and took the six-thirty train to Caltanissetta, where he spent a couple of hours at the courthouse in his usual searches through the criminal files. In this task he had the assistance of the court clerk, Fiasconaro, to whom he did not disclose his real identity.

The detective returned to Palermo early in the afternoon. At five o'clock, possibly after having seen the individuals with whom he had had an appointment for four, he returned to the Hôtel de France. Before he went up to his room he bought a copy of *Il Giornale di Sicilia*.

That day all the papers had big headlines on the outcome of the voting on the previous Sunday. Giolitti's victory, already indicated in the first balloting, had turned into a landslide. In southern Italy alone the Premier/Minister of the Interior had succeeded in carrying two hundred of his supporters into office with him. Naturally, in accordance with his habit, Giolitti had not overly concerned himself with the delicacies either in his choice of candidates or in the methods to be employed for their election. Prefects and police commissioners, ex-convicts and gambling-house operators had all done a first-rate job. Indeed, it should not be overlooked that it was just after these 1909 elections that a young Socialist deputy named Gaetano Salvemini* wrote his famous essay entitled *The Prime Ministry of the Underworld.*

_____

*One of the most incorruptible men in Italian public life; a firm anti-Fascist who went into exile early, later taught at Harvard, and became a noted historian.—Translator.

Giolitti himself was elected from three districts in Sicily although he had never put a foot on the island. In Palermo the Honorable Palizzolo, still linked to the monarchist-Crispi group, was soundly trounced by Giolitti's man, Di Stefano, who got 1981 votes to Palizzolo's 125. In Palermo's Second District, Pecoraro, the Catholic candidate, defeated Empedocle Restivo, and in the Third District Pietro di Trabia was elected. In Bivona Don Vito Cascio Ferro's protege, the Honorable Domenico De Michele Ferrantelli, won a reelection that was virtually a plebiscite.

After a quick look at the newpaper, Petrosino plunged himself into his work. He made typewritten copies of some of the penal certificates that he had got in Caltanissetta and then prepared notes for the next day. He had brought with him from New York a little notebook containing the list of criminals on whose backgrounds he wanted to collect material with which to launch proceedings for their deportation. That evening he added a name to the bottom of the list in a hasty script: "Vito Cascio Ferro, born in Sambuca Zabut, resident of Bisaquino, Province of Palermo, dreaded criminal."

Why did Petrosino add this note? What reason could have impelled him to launch an investigation of someone who, already living in Italy, had no occasion to figure in a list of persons to be deported from the United States? Perhaps he intended to denounce Don Vito to the Italian police because of the "barrel murder"? The question must remain unanswered.

At about six o'clock in the evening the storm that had been threatening for twenty-four hours made a dramatic entrance. It rained in sheets for more than an hour, with much thunder and lightning. At seven-thirty the rain suddenly stopped. Petrosino took his hat and his umbrella, put on his coat, and left the hotel to go to the Cafè Oreto for dinner.

12. The Night of
March 12

ON FRIDAY EVENING, MARCH 12, 1909, Piazza Marina in Palermo was dark and deserted. The yellowish light of the weak gas lamps at its four corners was reflected in the muddy puddles left by the rain, and the outlines of the buildings framing the square could barely be distinguished. The Garibaldi Garden in the center of the square was a mass of blackness that threw sinister shadows on the sidewalks still wet from the rain. Everything was deep in silence. Only from the upper corner, where the Shukert Company's streetcars had their terminus, came the muted hum of voices as the passengers boarded the waiting car to seek shelter from the penetrating chill until the car should start.

His stout body well wrapped inside the big overcoat that fell almost to his feet, Joseph Petrosino covered the few hundred yards between the Hôtel de France and the Cafè Oreto at a brisk pace. The Oreto's bars were crowded with drinkers. The restaurant itself, in contrast, was almost empty, and the detective strode to his customary table in the corner, where he could sit with his back against the wall. From there he could keep an eye on the entire room.

He ordered his dinner immediately: pasta with tomato sauce, fish, fried potatoes, cheese with pepper, fruit, and a half-liter of wine. He had a good appetite. He had reached the cheese when two men entered the restaurant and looked around as if they were in search of someone. A waiter named Geraci saw them approach the detective, whom they seemed to know, and greet him deferentially. They remained standing while they spoke to him, and the conversation was very brief. Then Petrosino dismissed them with a wave that might have meant: "I'll be right with you."

When the two strangers had gone out, the detective quickly finished his dinner, asked for the check, which amounted to 2.70 lire, and left three lire on the table; he did not wait for the change. Then he walked quickly to the door, buttoning his overcoat as he went.

It was eight-forty-five.

Once outside, Petrosino did not turn left, as he usually did, to take the shortest way to the hotel; he walked straight ahead and began to follow the fence round the Garibaldi Garden, as if he meant to pace the entire perimeter of the square. Obviously he was heading for a point that had been agreed upon with the two strangers. He was to walk exactly six-hundred-and-sixty feet.

About five minutes later, four pistol shots—three at one time, then a single shot—shattered the silence that cloaked Piazza Marina. The shots came from the corner that faced the church of San Giuseppe dei Miracoli, about a hundred feet from the streetcar terminus. Unbelievably enough, of all the waiting passengers the only one who ran to the scene of the shooting was a sailor. The others either stayed where they were or fled in the opposite direction. The courageous sailor was twenty-one-year-old Alberto Car-

della of Ancona, a member of the crew of the naval vessel
Calabria that had been at anchor in the port of Palermo for several
days.

Cardella was therefore the first person to grasp what had happened and, subsequently, the only one to offer worthwhile testimony. In those few seconds that it took him to reach the scene of
the crime, the young man made mental notes of several important
details. He saw a stout man move away from the fence round
the garden and fall heavily to the ground, while two other men
burst from the shadows and fled in the direction of Palazzo Partanna, disappearing in the darkness of the inner courtyard from
which there were other outlets to the alleys behind it. The sailor
also heard the sound of a carriage being driven away.

For a few seemingly endless minutes, Cardella was alone with
the stocky body of a man he did not know, lying motionless on the
sidewalk outside the garden. Beside him there were an umbrella
and a large revolver. The victim's derby hat had rolled to the base
of a column for advertising posters, of which there were two:

> This evening, 12 March 1909, at
> 8 o'clock, at the Teatro Biondo
> first performance by
> Paule Silver
> the French star

and:

> Pure wool cushions
> 1.75 to 2 lire

Cardella was joined shortly by a medical officer from his ship,
the *Calabria*. The lieutenant examined the unknown's man's body
and, when he saw that there was nothing to be done for him, he
left, instructing the sailor to remain on guard.

Almost a quarter-hour later, a police official named Frasca,
accompanied by his assistant, Li Voti, and a lesser official, Scherma,
arrived. Later still, one Cosentino, an examining magistrate on the
public prosecutor's staff, arrived.

Meanwhile, as a result of a sudden break in the flow of gas to the street lights, Piazza Marina was plunged into total darkness. This incident (which, it was suspected, had been planned to expedite the killers' flight) temporarily prevented any on-the-spot investigation. A passerby had to be sent to buy candles for that purpose.

The dead man was wearing a black suit, black shoes, and a dark grey overcoat. Around his neck he wore a brown silk necktie, and in a pocket of his vest there was a gold watch on a gold chain. He had three gunshot wounds: one in the right shoulder, one in the throat and one in the right cheek. Later a bullet was found in the fabric of his jacket. In view of the position of the wounds, it seemed clear that the man had been attacked not from the back but from the front, at close range, by persons who stood facing him as he was backed up against the iron fence.

No one present could identify the victim, who—as the police report put it—"had the appearance of a rich and elegant foreigner." Only after the body had been searched did Cosentino, the examining magistrate, discover that this was Joseph Petrosino.

The search, which was entrusted to the sailor Cardella, was most meticulous. In the right vest pocket he found a piece of paper with the number "6824" written on it in ink. Other pockets contained a checkbook issued by the Banca Commerciale; and one fifty-lire and four five-lire banknotes. There were a number of envelopes addressed to various prominent persons in Palermo including the Mayor, Senator De Martino; Enrico Ghilardi, Captain of the Port; Cutrera, the representative of the public-safety forces; and Grillone, a sergeant in the municipal police. The envelopes, which were still sealed, contained letters of introduction signed by one *L. Bonanno, merchant, 42 Stone St., Room 906, New York,* which Petrosino had not yet presented to the addressees. Cardella also found thirty of the detective's business cards; the letter of introduction from Leonardi, the head of the police; a notebook containing names of many offenders including the final addition of Vito Cascio Ferro; some memoranda on work to be done in the future; a picture postcard addressed to Mrs. Petrosino (on which was written

"A kiss for you and my little girl, who has spent three months far from her daddy"); and, finally, the detective's New York police badge, with the number 285.

The news that the dead man was the famous detective spread through the city. Commissioner Ceola, who had taken a box at the Teatro Biondo in order to admire Paule Silver, the French star, left the theater in the middle of the show and hurried to the scene of the crime.

At first the discovery of the big revolver, which was of Belgian make and from which one bullet had been fired, gave rise to the theory that Petrosino had attempted a desperate defense. Indeed, it was argued that it was he who had fired the fourth shot that had been heard separately from the three others. But this hypothesis was discarded when, after his hotel room had been searched, his Smith & Wesson was found in his suitcase. So Joseph Petrosino had gone out unarmed that night; apparently he had the utmost confidence in whoever had laid the fatal ambush.

While the detective's body, still under guard by Cardella, the sailor, lay awaiting removal to the morgue of the Rotoli Cemetery, questioning of the few witnesses rounded up at the scene was beginning in police headquarters. It was a wasted effort.

Gaetano Casalis and Giuseppe Morello, ticket collectors for the streetcar line, were the first to be examined. Casalis admitted that he had heard the shots. "But I didn't see anything," he very quickly added. Morello was still less informative: "I didn't hear anything," he said; "I just saw a man and a girl running off, very frightened, but I didn't know why."

The ticket collectors were followed by two motormen, Giovanni Battista Salerno and Lorenzo Rossiglione. Salerno acknowledged that he had heard shots, but nothing else. Rossiglione, on the other hand, said he had seen flashes. "But I didn't even hear the shots," he clarified.

An off-duty Carabiniere, on his own initiative, arrested one Luigi Schillaci, whose job was lubricating the streetcars and who seemed to know something about the two persons who had been seen running away. But when he got to Police Headquarters he suffered a sudden loss of memory. "I didn't see anything and I didn't hear anything," he insisted.

Since Cardella, the sailor, kept repeating that he had seen the murderers fleeing in the direction of Palazzo Partanna, the building's concierges, Giovanno Battista Patricola and Nunzia Lo Cascio, were brought in for questioning. But they too firmly denied having seen or heard anything.

The first important arrest made by the police was that of Paolo Palazzotto. He had been seen that evening with Ernesto Militano in the Cafè Oreto. Furthermore, his name was on Petrosino's list, with those of his brothers Domenico and Michele, well-known members of the "Black Hand" in Brooklyn.

Palazzotto was snatched out of bed in his room at two o'clock in the morning. "I was home all day because I wasn't feeling well," he said over and over. Then his position was made worse by the testimony of a certain Enrico Fazio, who had heard him making vague threats against Petrosino as the detective was leaving the American consulate in Piazza Castelnuovo.

Ernesto Militano was arrested later. The police had trouble recognizing him because he had chosen that very morning to shave off his celebrated moustache.

"Why did you get rid of your moustache?" he was asked.

"Because my woman likes me better without." And that was all that they could get out of him.

Meanwhile Commissioner Ceola was seeing to it that Bishop, the consul, and the Ministry of the Interior were notified. Cavalier Poli, in command of the Mobile Brigade, set in motion a major roundup of all Sicilians recently expelled from America who might have reason to kill Petrosino. During that night—March 13—considerable progress was made in the investigation; so much, indeed, that there was reason to suppose that the identification of the killers was imminent. Some extremely important evidence was supplied by Tommaso Chiusa, a thirty-one-year-old native of Partinico, who was employed as a porter in the building at 8 Piazza Castelnuovo.

On the preceding morning Chiusa had taken his little daughter to the Garibaldi Garden, where he had recognized Carlo Costantino and Antonio Passananti sitting on a bench. This had surprised him, because he had thought they were still in America. Now, since the murder of Petrosino, his surprise had become suspicion. For this reason he had made up his mind to tell the police.

As a matter of fact, the police were not unaware of the return of Costantino and Passananti under false names. The agent-in-charge in Partinico, Cavalier Battioni, had drawn up a very detailed report on the matter. From this report, which also included the text of the mysterious cable sent by Costantino to Morelli, it appeared that, though the two men owned a thriving liquor business in New York, they had returned unexpectedly to Partinico. Questioned by Cavalier Battioni for the reasons for their surprising repatriation, they had told him they had been forced to leave New York to escape certain Jewish moneylenders who were insisting on immediate repayment of loans. This statement, however, seemed to contradict the fact that they were manifestley rich. The agent-in-charge added that, on the basis of confidential information, he had learned that a few days before their arrival Don Vito Cascio Ferro had gone to Partinico to get news of them. Costantino and Passananti then went to Bisaquino to visit the notorious Mafioso.

This report, which had not occasioned any particular interest until now, made it possible for Baldassare Ceola to perceive the outline of an international plot against the life of the American detective. He immediately sent some of his men to Partinico, where Carlo Costantino was found at home. When he was asked what he had done the night before, he was unable to come up with a convincing story. Antonio Passananti, however, was not found. He had left Partinico on March 12 and had not come back.

The search for the killers continued to widen. Within less than forty-eight hours after the crime, the investigators had focused their attention on fifteen persons, all of whom had come back from the United States and all of whom were connected with the Mafia or the "Black Hand." They were Palazzotto; Militano; Salvatore Seminara, forty years old; Camillo Pericò, forty-four; Francesco Pericó, forty-six; Pasquale Enea, forty; Costantino, thirty-five; Passananti, thirty; Giovanno Ruisi, forty; Giuseppe Bonfardeci, twenty-eight; Giuseppe Fatta, thirty-three; Giovanni Dazzò, thirty-six; Giovanni Battista Finazzo, twenty-eight; Gaspare Tedeschi, forty-five; and Vito Cascio Ferro, forty-seven. Of all of them, only Vito Cascio Ferro and Passananti had not yet been picked up.

The first New York newspaper to publish an exclusive story of the murder of Petrosino was the *New York Herald*. One of its reporters knocked at Adelina Petrosino's door at 233 Elizabeth Street at two o'clock in the morning.

"Have you any news of your husband?" he asked.

"No, why? What's happened to him?"

"You don't know anything, then?"

"No. O God! Something's happened. Has he been killed?"

"No, no, just hurt . . . I thought you knew."

The reporter said nothing more and rushed off. In tears, Adelina went upstairs, her daughter in her arms, to her brother Louis. He sent for Doctor Asselta, who had been a friend of the policeman for some twenty-five years, and turned his sister over to the doctor. Then he went to police headquarters.

No one there, of course, would believe what Louis Saulino had to say. "Petrosino dead? Impossible . . . Another of those reporters with a good imagination . . . It's probably some trick the lieutenant's up to. This isn't the first time there've been rumors of his death . . . Do you remember that time when . . ."

It was dawn when Louis Saulino left police headquarters. He was now certain that the whole thing was some malicious joke. But when he was out in the street he heard the newsboys hawking the *New York Herald* and already announcing the famous detective's death at the top of their lungs.

After a glance at the paper, which had a very detailed story cabled by its Rome correspondent, Saulino went back to police headquarters. "Do you still think it's some hoax?" he asked, throwing the paper down on a desk.

At this point the desk officer on night duty decided it would be appropriate to telephone Deputy Commissioner Woods (General Bingham was in Washington but was scheduled to return during the day). Woods came on the run. Shaking his head, he read the newspaper story and murmured, as if to himself: "It's impossible, it's impossible."

Until ten o'clock that morning Police Headquarters waited in a state of tension. Then came the cable from the consul in Palermo that provided official confirmation. It read:

> Palermo, Italy, 12 March 1909 Petrosino killed revolver center city tonight. Killers unknown. Martyr's death.
>
>   Bishop, consul.

Later Woods agreed to make a statement for the press, although by now the reporters knew more than he did. General Bingham, however, shut himself in his room in the Hotel Iroquois as soon as he returned to New York, and refused to see anyone. His secretary, Daniel Slattery, announced that for the present the Commissioner would not have any statement to make.

The sense of loss at the Italian policeman's death was general. The newspapers devoted more space to his murder than they had given to President McKinley's. For a long time there was no talk of anything else in New York, and naturally the press campaign against Italian immigration was resumed with vehemence. Once again there were densely written articles under such titles as LET'S THROW THEM OUT! None of these indignant essayists, however, seemed to recall that "the loyal defender of New York," "the Number One enemy of the 'Black Hand,' " "the heroic Lieutenant Petrosino" was, when one came down to it, an Italian himself.

A fierce attack on the Italian police was also launched at once in New York. Police headquarters in Palermo was accused of minimal cooperation and also of complicity with the murderers by reason of its refusal to provide the American police with a detailed report on the incident. (In actuality, following normal practice, Commissioner Ceola had been obliged to send this report through diplomatic channels, and that was the reason for the delay in its delivery.) General Bingham in particular kept this campaign at a high pitch, presumably with the aim of throwing all the responsibility on his colleagues on the other side of the ocean. Petrosino's closest collaborator, Antonio Vachris (who in the interim had been promoted to lieutenant and was expected to succeed Petrosino), declared quite baldly that his chief "had certainly been betrayed by the Palermo police." And Assistant District Attorney Francis L. Corrao made this statement available to the press:

The Italian government must be held largely responsible for Petrosino's death. There is no doubt that his murder was ordered and planned here in New York, but the death sentence was carried out with soldierly discipline by the Sicilian Mafia. From what I saw and heard during my recent trip to Italy, I have no doubt that the public officials in Sicily are hand in glove with the Mafia. I had the impression that the Italian government cooperates in keeping the organization going. Until the community of interest between the heads of the Mafia and the police has been destroyed, there will be no end to the reign of the Mafia in Sicily.

As soon as he had been told of his old associate's death, former President Theodore Roosevelt also wanted to make a statement. "I cannot find words," he said, "to express my profound grief. Petrosino was a great and good man, a loyal and valiant patriot. I knew him and respected him for many years. He never knew what fear was. He was a man worth knowing. I am sincerely grieved by the death of my friend, Joe."

In those days of "collective hysteria," as the impartial Arthur Brisbane was constrained to call it in the *New York Journal,* the American press put forward illogical theories on the mysterious affair. Some papers insinuated that the crime had been committed by Italian anarchists, in combination with the Mafiosi, emphasizing the fact that Petrosino had been as bitter an enemy of the one as of the other. In this connection the London correspondent of *The New York Times* felt obliged to interview Enrico Malatesta in order to get his view of the Palermo murder. The anarchist leader, however, showed a total lack of interest in what had happened to the Italian-American detective. "I can say only," he confined himself to stating, "that, in the light of what I have had to suffer because of the police, Petrosino's death leaves me absolutely indifferent."

The press in America, however, continued to follow "the anarchist trail." For example, readers were given detailed reports for
days on the hunt that was being conducted by the London police
for an anarchist named Angelo Caruso, the owner of a mangy dog
that he had named Petrosino in memory of an ugly encounter with
the detective in the "undesirable aliens' pen" on Ellis Island. (Later,
when Caruso was tracked down, it was of course found that he had
had absolutely nothing to do with the crime.)

At the heart of the violent anti-Italian newspaper campaign that
had been unleashed in America, however, was the exceptionally
savage bill of indictment drawn up by a writer named White and
published in a respected paper, the *Ledger,* which published it on
Sunday, March 21. The article, which provoked a sharp diplomatic
incident, said among other things:

Petrosino's killers will never be brought to justice. It is just as well
that the people of New York resign themselves to this fact.

Nor is there the slightest likelihood that any of the most important
documents in his possession at the time of his death—papers dealing
with his investigations of the criminal records of Italians in America—
will ever reach Mulberry Street. In fact, they were taken from his
body and from his room immediately after his death by the Palermo
police, who, it can safely be assumed, have done and will do everything
in their power to protect not only the murderers of the detective but
all those Italians in America whose criminal records were in fact the
objects of his investigations.

This does not necessarily mean that the Palermo police were active
accomplices of Petrosino's killers, but it does mean that they neither
intend nor dare to lift a finger against them. That would be contrary
to their peculiar sense of honor and duty, besides the fact that—as they
well know—it would bring all kinds of harm to themselves and their
families. Similar influences will affect the officials charged with throwing light on the case, and it is doubtful whether any of the persons
arrested is in fact connected with the tragedy.

To judge on the basis of past experience, it is probable that the
men arrested are completely innocent and that their more or less brief
imprisonment is in fact the result of their having aroused the anger
of the Mafia, which is taking advantage of the opportunity to punish

them and teach them a lesson about its power. These people can consider themselves lucky if the Mafia does not decide to produce false evidence that would make them appear responsible for Petrosino's death; in that case it would be men who were absolutely innocent, if not of any crime, certainly of this killing in particular, who would pay.

All this may sound strange, and I am well aware that these statements will be considered ridiculous by the Italian officials who represent their government abroad. In fact, they know very well that it would cost them their jobs to admit that such things as the Mafia and the Camorra exist. They are taught, instead, to insist that such secret societies and associations for criminal purposes have long since become nothing but myths, surviving only in the imaginations of foreigners and fanciful newspaper men who depend for their living on the invention of storybook plots.

But Senator Costanzo Codringhi, who comes from northern Italy and who, because of his integrity and courage, was appointed personally by the late King Umberto I as his High Commissioner in Sicily for the express purpose of driving out the Mafia, was compelled to retire by political forces even more powerful than his sovereign. Codringhi, however, did not retire before he had become convinced of the futility of his assignment, since not only was the entire population of the island united in defense of the Mafia, but the Mafia could command the support and good will of high local officials and even of the Cabinet, imposing its influence and its orders on every Sicilian deputy and senator in the National Legislature. Senator Codringhi came out of his seclusion a few years ago to testify in the trial of Palizzolo for the murder of Marquis Emanuele Notarbartolo, and on that occasion he spoke of the Mafia, under oath, as follows:

"It exerts its poisonous influence on everything in Sicily. Everyone is afraid of it . . . And, in order to protect their own property and ther own safety, the people are compelled to submit to its orders . . . Its power knows no barrier even in confrontation with the government. Read the description of the Bravi in *I Promessi Sposi** and you will have a vague idea of the power of the Mafia."

In the meantime, the *New York Herald* had not missed the chance to proclaim the superiority of its own "exclusive dispatches."

---

*A classic of Italian fiction by Alessandro Manzoni (1785–1873).—Translator.

This is its "lead" to a long story on the investigations under way in Palermo that appeared on March 14:

The *New York Herald* has scored the journalistic triumph of recent months with its story of the murder of Lieutenant Petrosino. No other morning paper carried a line on the crime. Only the evening papers picked up the story, giving it top headlines. Even in Police Headquarters no one had any knowledge of the murder until ten o'clock yesterday morning, when a cablegram arrived from Mr. Bishop, the United States consul in Palermo.

Curiously, not one American newspaper pointed out at the time the indiscretion of Commissioner Bingham's public disclosure (another "exclusive" published by the *Herald*) of Petrosino's secret mission to Italy. At the same time, Bingham's refusal to say anything for publication about the policeman's death does indicate that the head of New York's police must have felt a certain constraint.

Although the seriousness of the indiscretion was not stressed by the American press, the Italian police (who also felt obliged now to evade responsibility as much as possible) were quick to criticize that shocking imprudence with the utmost severity. They were echoed by the Italian press. Since Italians did not know that it had been Bingham himself who had provided the information, the suspicion was voiced that the story in the *Herald* on Petrosino's secret journey had been specifically intended to sound the alarm to the Sicilian Mafia.

In connection with this volley of charges between the two police forces, an American in Palermo at that time, A. H. Russel, wrote a long letter to Commissioner Bingham. It is still extant in the files of the New York Police Department.

Palermo, March 17, 1909

Dear Sir:

Perhaps what I am writing to you about the Petrosino case will tell you nothing that you do not know when you receive this letter, but the latest issue of the Paris edition of the *New York Herald* reports that the police officials in Palermo are not keeping you informed.

The clipping that I enclose, which is dated the 14th of this

month, repeats almost word for word the story as it appeared in
Il Mattino of Naples on the same day, but in fact it was printed
the night before. I am also sending you some later excerpts from
articles in *Il Mattino*.

Great bewilderment is expressed over the fact that the "Black
Hand" was familiar with Petrosino's movements, the more so in
that he was traveling under a false name. As for the *Herald,* it
claims great merit for its discovery and for the triumph that it
scored in being first with the news. But, while it may deserve
praise for this from the journalistic point of view, I believe that
it should be harshly criticized because it was in fact the *Herald*
that made the secret disclosure of Petrosino's planned trip to
Sicily a matter of public knowledge.

The copy of the *Herald* that I am sending you, dated March 14,
Paris edition, contains, obviously as proof of its journalistic enterprise, the text of a story of February 20 that reveals everything
about the planned journey. It did not require any special brilliance
in men of evil intentions, whatever their organization might actually be, to follow Petrosino after such a warning.

Since it is impossible to believe that he wanted to have publicity
about his journey and then assumed another name, it seems likely
to me that the story was blurted out by some trusted person in
your secret service. In short, the same thing happened that happens with American movements in war, which, particularly if they
are secret, are always announced by our newspapers in time to
warn the enemy. It would be much better to follow the methods
of the Japanese . . .

The immediate and complete account given by the Naples newspaper struck me because the Italian press is not distinguished for
the timeliness of its news nor for the accuracy and completeness
of its information. It seemed almost as if the news had been given
out in advance this time, ready for publication. And when the
New York Herald printed the same story, I wondered whether,
in the advanced development of its "initiative," it had not gone
to the extreme of having its correspondents follow Petrosino to
Palermo.

In Italy there has been harsh criticism of the inefficiency shown
by the local police in this case, since their officials must certainly
have been in communication with Petrosino, and, even if he did

not want a bodyguard, elementary precautionary measures could have prevented the crime.

The reasons for the policeman's trip were precisely those stated by the *Herald* on February 20, and it is impossible that the police of Palermo could have given the reporters details on the detective's identity if they had not been in close contact with those reporters and, perhaps, with the murderers. Who knows whether the *Herald* correspondent too was not a member of the gang?

> Yours very truly,
> A. H. Russel
> Major, U.S. Army, retired

Naturally, the retired major did not know that it was Bingham himself who had informed the *Herald,* and no doubt he expected some recognition for his laudable communication, as well, perhaps, as a request that he join the investigation. So he must have been quite disappointed when he received this very frigid reply:

> New York, April 1, 1909
>
> Dear Mr. Russel:
>   The Police Commissioner has asked me to inform you that he has received your letter and its enclosures. Your information will be given proper attention.
>
> > (Signature illegible)
> > Assistant to the Commissioner

On the night of March 18 the remains of Joseph Petrosino were moved from the morgue of the Rotoli Cemetery to that of the Hostel for the Poor in Corso Calatafimi. There Professor Giacinto Vetere—who had come from Naples for the purpose—proceeded to embalm the body, using a secret technique of his own devising. It took him about four hours. Later Petrosino was laid in a specially lined coffin in preparation for the long journey to New York.

The following day was St. Joseph's day, the policeman's name day. That morning, in the church connected with the hostel, a funeral service was held, attended by eighty city policemen under the command of Major Crapa. The bier was covered with wreaths and flowers sent by the Mayor, Senator Di Martino; the Public

Prosecutor's Office; and Palermo Police Headquarters. At nine o'clock the large crowd that was waiting outside the church was admitted and allowed to pay its respects before the coffin. The tribute continued without interrpution until two o'clock in the afternoon, when the funeral procession formed ranks. It was to proceed through Corso Calatafimi, Piazza Indipendenza, Corso Vittorio Emanuele, Quattro Cantoni, Via Maqueda, Via Ruggero Settimo, and Piazza Castelnuovo. The crowd was huge; schools, offices and shops had closed for the occasion to allow maximum participation by the populace. The ceremonies were directed by Bishop, the American consul, who seemed extremely nervous. Much curiosity was aroused by the presence of a motion-picture crew, headed by a cameraman called Lucarelli, hired to record the scene at the request of the United States Embassy.

At the head of the procession marched Carabinieri in dress uniform; they were followed by the night watch, with flag, and then by the Mayor, Commissioner Ceola, Bishop, a representative from the Cercle des Étrangers (Foreigners' Club) of Palermo, other municipal authorities, members of Parliament, the municipal band, the firemen, the customs guards, the port police, and the city police. The coffin, borne in a hearse pulled by six black horses, was wrapped in an American flag and escorted by eight Carabinieri. Behind the bier the rest of the procession stretched over a distance of more than a mile, and the rear was brought up by members of the Garibaldi Society, wearing red shirts and carrying a flag. The only city official missing was De Seta, the Prefect, who had sent Cavalier De Lanchenal to represent him.

At about five-thirty, a strange thing happened when the procession arrived in Piazza Castelnuovo. According to the plans, funeral orations were to have been delivered by the Assistant Public Prosecutor, Nuccio Grillo, and Cavalier De Lanchenal. But when the two speakers were already on the platform set up for the occasion, Bishop, the consul, was observed in excited conversation with the driver of the hearse. A second later there was the crack of a whip, and the horses, urged on by the driver's voice as well, unexpectedly set off at a gallop in the direction of the harbor.

The perplexing flight of the hearse naturally caused a great sensation. A rumor immediately circulated that this had been a stratagem to prevent a demonstration inspired by a group of anarchists. But the truth was quite different: Bishop had decided on this action simply in order to eliminate the planned funeral orations.

At the harbor, the coffin was placed "in bond" and signed for by Settimo Codiglione, a clerk. It remained in storage until March 23, when it was loaded aboard the British steamer *Slavonia* of the Cunard Line, bound for New York.

The ship arrived in New York on April 9 and a funeral service was held three days later in the old St. Patrick's Church in Mott Street, where Bishop Lavalle, an old friend of the detective's, celebrated the mass and delivered the eulogy. He concluded by saying that Petrosino was "a man with the blazon of nobility not on a parchment but in his heart."

No prominent American had ever received so great a tribute as the homage that New Yorkers paid to the Italian-American lieutenant. A huge throng marched in the procession. The day was declared an official holiday and flags were flown at half-staff on all public buildings in the city.

Pallbearers carried the coffiin from the church to the offices of the Republican Party in Lafayette Street. The bearers were the closest of the dead man's associates. They placed the coffin in the hearse as the police band played "Nearer, My God, to Thee," followed by Verdi's "Requiem."

All the city's officials took part in the procession. The hearse— which was followed by the widow and intimate friends, one thousand mounted and foot patrolmen, two thousand school children, sixty Italian associations in uniform, and a crowd of about two hundred thousand—moved through Broadway, Mercer Street, Fourteenth Street, Twenty-third Street, Thirty-fourth Street, and Forty-second Street to Fifth Avenue. The march lasted five and a half hours, during the whole of which the center of New York was immobilized. From Fifth Avenue, where the marchers disbanded, the hearse—followed by two companies of mounted police, the guard of honor, and a number of carriages bearing the widow and the municipal officials—went on to Calvary Cemetery. There, after another moving ceremony, the coffin was entombed at the foot of a small stone inscribed: "Erected by Adelina Petrosino in memory of her beloved husband, Joseph Petrosino, who died on March 12, 1909, at the age of forty-nine years."

Americans' grief at the loss of the famous detective was widespread and deep. Petrosino was also honored in the United States Senate. Then, when it was learned that the detective had died poor, New York showed great generosity toward his family. Ten thousand dollars were collected by public subscription and the Board of Aldermen and the Board of Estimate awarded his widow an annual pension of a thousand dollars.

Unfortunately, it was not only expressions of sympathy that came to the widow at that time. She also received many letters from the Black Hand, containing obscure threats against her and her daughter. Therefore she decided to give up her old home at 233 Lafayette Street in order to live with her brother, Vincent, at 623 Fiftieth Avenue in Brooklyn. This house, in which the detective's widow died in 1957 at the age of eighty, is still occupied by her daughter, Adelina, the guardian of all the mementos (including the gold watch from Giolitti) left by her father.

13. Commissioner Ceola's Investigation

FOR SEVERAL WEEKS BALDASSARE CEOLA, who had been Police
Commissioner in Palermo for less than two years, found himself
at the eye of the hurricane unleashed by the Petrosino case. Not
even the assassination of Umberto I in Monza had so upset his
nervous system. Harried by ever-more-urgent dispatches from the
Premier (parsimonious though he was, Giolitti even authorized
Ceola to offer a reward of ten thousand lire to anyone who provided valid clues leading to the solution of the case); beaten down
by inspectors general of the public-safety forces who dropped on
him from Rome; nagged by Bishop, the consul, and Griscom, the
ambassador, who were constantly calling for the arrest of the
criminals; he had also to hold his own against the Italian and
foreign press, neither of which ever let by a single opportunity
to hint maliciously at his presumed complicity with the Mafia.

In spite of all this, Baldassare Ceola did a good job. He was an honest, capable official. Born in Pergine in the Province of Trento in 1846, he had made a brilliant career. Appointed Commissioner in Milan in 1899, he had been promoted to Inspector General of Public Safety in 1905. In Palermo, where he had been serving since 1907, he had already made great progress in purging Mafia infiltrations from police circles.

He directed the investigations into the Petrosino murder intelligently and methodically. If his efforts were not crowned with success, the reasons are to be sought in circles other than those of the Palermo Police Headquarters.

From the very start of the investigations, Ceola set out three hypotheses before his colleagues:

1. Petrosino was killed by Paolo Palazzotto or other "undesirables" whose intentions were to get vengeance both for harsh treatment undergone in America and for deportation from that country.
2. Petrosino was sentenced to death by the Mafia in order to prevent him from carrying out his plans to block access to the United States for Sicilian criminals.
3. Petrosino was killed on a contract from the Black Hand which, because of the penal certificates that the detective was collecting, feared the expulsion of many of its members from America.

For several days the investigators worked feverishly along these three lines, but, as soon as he had analyzed their early findings, Ceola concluded that the three original hypotheses could be merged into one. In sum, Petrosino was killed for a number of reasons that included personal vengence, the survival of the "black bridge" between Palermo and New York, and the rescue of the Black Hand chiefs threatened with deportation.

"Lieutenant Petrosino's arrival in Palermo," Ceola wrote in one of his reports, "frightened too many people and threatened too many interests. For this reason a regular international coalition was organized against him. Furthermore, the fatal ambush carefully set up by the murderers, with the assistance of false confidential agents who succeeded in convicing the ingenuous detective that he could manage without the cooperation of the police, clearly shows that the preparation of the crime must be laid to an association of criminals possessing substantial resources."

Baldassare Ceola had arrived at this conclusion on the basis of a series of deductions derived from the earliest findings and also from information received from the United States. Now, indeed, Ceola was in a position to answer the classic question that he had asked himself from the moment when he had stood beside the policeman's body on the sidewalk in Piazza Marina: *Who would gain from this?*

The policeman's death would naturally benefit the Mafia, which felt threatened in its plans for expansion in America; but there was remarkable profit also for a great many individuals.

Petrosino's death was very much to the benefit of Vito Cascio Ferro, for whom Petrosino's arrival and the possible reopening of the "barrel murder," for which he had still to answer before the American courts, could have meant the end of his peaceful, profitable *respectability.*

It was to the benefit of Giuseppe Morello, Giuseppe Fontana, Ignazio Lupo, and other leaders of the Black Hand against whom extradition proceedings had been begun. After Petrosino's visit to Palermo, they would certainly have been carried to a successful conclusion.

The murder also profited Paolo Palazzotto and all the other "undesirable aliens" who longed to return to the United States and might have thought that they would make this more likely by eliminating the man who represented their major obstacle.

As for Carlo Costantino and Antonino Passananti, Commissioner Ceola was still uncertain what parts they had played. They might have been killers sent to Palermo for this purpose; equally, they might have been run-of-the-mill criminals who, having come home to enjoy the loot that they had accumulated, had taken part in the crime in the conviction that Petrosino had come to Sicily to arrest them.

The doubts remaining in Ceola's mind as to the reasons and

modus operandi of the crime were in large measure cleared by three anonymous letters that he received from New York. These letters are of considerable importance, even with due regard to the reservations imposed by the absence of signatures. They were written in the period immediately after the murder (in fact, the first is postmarked March 13, so that it must have been written only a few hours after the disclosure of the detective's death). In consequence we can eliminate the hypothesis that the writers were influenced by the various theories put forward later by the press. The first letter read:

New York, March 13, 1909

Illustrissimo signor Questore,

On you falls the responsibility for the murder of poor Petrosino, because you, knowing his lofty mission, never had him escorted by your subordinates.

That way a tremendous catastrophe would have been avoided.

In any case, what's done is done. I only wanted to tell you that the organizers of this murder were: Giuseppe Morello, head of the "Black Hand." Giuseppe Fontana, murderer of Marquis di Notarbartolo. Ignazio Milone. Pietro Inzerillo, owner of the Star of Italy, a dive. And the two Terranova brothers, stepbrothers of Giuseppe Morello. All in the "Black Hand," all very dangerous.

The job was turned over by them to their colleague, Vito Cascio Ferro of Bisaquino, whose photograph Petrosino always carried on him because he wanted to arrest him.

All this is as much as I can say. Secrecy and nothing but.

An Honest Sicilian

P.S. I have written another letter like this one to the Minister of the Interior.

Whatever importance one may choose to give to this information, it is worthwhile noting that it contains a specific charge against Vito Cascio Ferro whose name not only had not yet appeared in the newspapers but had not even been given any thought by the police.

Then, three days later, the same writer sent a second letter to Ceola:

New York, March 16, 1909

Signor Questore,

I am confirming my registered letter of a few days ago. Note that the plot to murder poor Petrosino was made in New York and the orders were sent to Vito Cascio Ferro of Bisaquino and Ignazio Lupo of Palermo.* These two criminals were implacable enemies of Petrosino and were the terror of New York.

The plot was worked out in New York and the chief organizers are: Giuseppe Morello, brother-in-law of Ignazio Lupo, Gioacchino Lima, also a brother-in-law of Morello, Ignazio Milone and the Terranova brothers. They are the most terrible killers in New York, having killed people even in broad daylight. The police know all these gentlemen well. They contributed fifty dollars each to send two killers to murder Petrosino, but it seems that at the last minute they changed their minds.

Pay attention to me: follow this road and you'll get to the goal. Don't accuse others. May I end in the poorhouse if I am not writing you the truth. Today in New York it is no mystery to anybody. Many members of the "Black Hand" are boasting about it.

An Honest Sicilian

This second letter contained a new element that also could not be attributed to the writer's imagination or the newspapers' influence: that was the mention of the two killers who were to have sailed for Italy. At that point the papers had not said anything about Costantino and Passananti, and therefore the anonymous correspondent must obviously have heard rumors that were circulating in Little Italy.

Meanwhile another anonymous letter, from a different source, but equally intriguing, was sent from America to the police commissioner of Palermo. It was written in dialect, curiously, even though the writer showed a certain skill in the use of language. He was probably a reasonably educated Italian-American who used the dialect he had learned from his parents. His letter read:

---

*Lupo had indeed disappeared from New York at this period, but he was later traced to Paterson, New Jersey.—Author.

Brooklyn, March 16, 1909

Signuri Questuri,

I am sorry about Petrosino's death because he was a too good guy, and therefore I want you to know that a certain Paolo Orlannu was a too much enemy of Petrosino he is the capo [chief] in the Mafia in Brooklyn while he was the chief of the Mafia of Tunis before. They sent him away from there and he came to Brooklyn and had his house at 32 in Hopkins stritta [street]. He had him killed by two Partinicans who disappeared from Brooklyn because they went bankrupt and took away a lot of money. Petrosino was looking for them. They left all the wine in their store for this Paulo [sic] Orlannu and if you don't want to believe me write to Tunis and you'll see that it is the truth. You can write to Brooklyn for the two Partinicans whose names are A. Passananti and the other Carlo Costantino, Savannah 593, Husking a.v.

An Honored Sicilian

With the letter—in which the two killers alluded to in the other letter were cited for the first time by name—there was a scrap of a newspaper published in Philadelphia, with an orange label on which was stamped "A. Passananti, 593 Finslimg."

These three anonymous letters were the only ones, out of the thousands that were sent from all parts of the world, that the police took seriously. It should also be pointed out that, because of the distance involved, they reached their destination on April 1—that is, when Ceola believed that he had completed his investigation. Hence they did not reveal any new facts but, rather, confirmed the theories held by the police.

By now, in fact, the Police Commissioner of Palermo was convinced that he had solved the case. He had come to the conclusion that the "brains" of the conspiracy must have been Vito Cascio Ferro, assisted by Carlo Costantino and Antonino Passananti. All three were friends and had been seen together before the murder. Furthermore, it was known that Costantino (in addition to the noted telegram to Morello: "I Lo Baido work Fontana") had communicated on other occasions with the head of the Black Hand. According to Ceola, it was Don Vito who had organized the murder, making the most of the availability of men and materials that resulted from his position as a Mafia chief. Ceola was also sure that the thirteen other criminals arrested by the police immediately after the crime had taken part in it, some by pretending to work with Petrosino, some by assisting the killers to flee, and some, finally, merely by creating confusion and sending the police after planted clues.

On April 2, 1909, when Baldassare Ceola sat down to put together his final report, two of his fifteen suspects were still missing: Antonino Passananti, who had dropped out of sight on the very evening of the murder, and Vito Cascio Ferro, who had disappeared from Bisaquino. Their absence, however, was evidence against them.

Here is the text of the report that the commissioner sent to the presiding officer of the Indictment Division of the Criminal Court of Palermo:

It was already long known to this headquarters that the very dangerous criminal Vito Cascio Ferro, son of Accursio and the former Santa Ippolito, born on 25 June 1862, was being sought by the police of New York as the murderer, with others, of one Benedetto Madonia, whose body, cut into pieces, was found in a barrel. Now, from information received from New York, it appears that Petrosino intended to visit the town of Bisaquino too, where Cascio Ferro resides. And, since he is notorious, also because *Il Giornale di Sicilia,* discussing the aforesaid crime at the time, referred to the charge made against Cascio Ferro (at that time identified by mistake as Cassa Ferro), and in addition because the case was being handled by Lieutenant Petrosino, it would not seem unlikely that the aforementioned official intended to go to Bisaquino specifically in order to look into the aforesaid criminal, whose name, moreover, appears clearly written in his notebook.

Cascio Ferro, whose record is enclosed, emigrated to America in 1901 in order to escape special surveillance and returned from there in 1904 (that is, after the commission of the "barrel murder"), occasioning astonishment by his sudden reappearance in Bisaquino. Now he is notorious for his connection with the so-called "upper Mafia"; he has extensive connections in the neighboring towns, as well as in the areas of Bivona, Sciacca and Palermo, where he controls the most dreaded criminals. He comes to this city frequently and remains here for several days. Although he has no visible means of support, he leads a very lavish life, going to theaters and cafés and gambling for very high stakes in the Civilian Club. Therefore it is believed that in his comings and goings, during which it is difficult to keep him under surveillance because of his most remarkable cunning, he is able to plan and execute his crimes with impunity.

Cascio Ferro would like to have it thought that his income is derived from his work as an agent or broker in the sale of agricultural products for the Honorable De Michele Ferrantelli and Baron Inglese, both of whom honor him with their friendship and protection.

In recent days, before the political elections, the hereinbeforementioned Cascio Ferro departed from Bisaquino and returned there on March 18, indicating that he had been employed in towns of the electoral districts of Burgio and Bivona in gathering support for the said Hon. De Michele's candidacy. Since then he has vanished again.

Since it has not been possible to ascertain accurately where he was on the day on which Petrosino was killed, and even granted that he was traveling in the towns above indicated for the reason heretofore mentioned, the possibility is not to be excluded that on the day of the crime he could have returned to Palermo in order to organize or even in order to carry it out himself, leaving again at once for Burgio in order to establish an alibi for himself. It is also known that, when he comes to Palermo, he stays sometimes at the Albergo Belvedere, in Piazza San Francesco, near Piazza Marina, but almost always, in order not to leave any sign of his presence, he stays with friends and protectors.

As for the other persons named in the two anonymous letters signed by "An Honest Sicilian," which have already been forwarded for your examination, I believe it is my duty to summarize the criminal records of some of the persons to whom the letters allude.

Giuseppe Fontana, a notorious Mafioso admonished and sentenced several times for highway robbery, abduction, etc., was directly accused as the chief organizer of the murder of Commendatore Notarbartolo. A subsequent emigrant to America, he is regarded by the local police as one of the most terrible of criminals. Three crimes are charged to him, and it is believed that he lives by extortion and blackmail. The police also believe that the bar owned by Fontana and Ignazio Milone in New York is a meeting place for members of the Black Hand. Proceedings for his expulsion from the United States have been under way for some time. It should be added, finally, that, although the penal certificate issued by this most honorable Tribunal shows only a single accusation, of which, moreover, he was acquitted for lack of evidence, according to the records of my office the charges lodged against Fontana appear to be much more numerous.

Giuseppe Morello, from Corleone, who emigrated to America several years ago, has been sentenced several times for making and distributing counterfeit banknotes. In America he has frequently been accused of serious crimes. I must add that, according to the Sub-Prefect of Corleone, Morello might well have been involved in the murder of Petrosino, the latter having come here in connection with the proceedings for the former's expulsion from America, which would certainly have taken place as soon as Petrosino had discovered the existence of a sentence to six years in prison imposed by the Messina court in 1894 and never served by Morello.

Ignazio Lupo, son of Rocco and of Onofria Saitta, thirty-two years old, of Palermo, is now being sought by the Italian police for the murder of a certain Salvatore Morello. Proceedings for his deportation are now being pressed by the American police. The other persons named in the two anonymous letters also correspond to offenders who are in positions analogous to those above mentioned.

Consequently, as I have already stated in my other reports, the motive for Petrosino's murder should be chiefly looked for in the tremendous fear that his previously announced arrival on this island must have produced among the numerous Sicilian criminals responsible for serious crimes, and thus far remaining unpunished, who have taken refuge in the United States, as well as among those who have fled from there to Italy in order to get beyond the reach of the American police.

To them, there can be no doubt, Petrosino's trip, of which the New York newspapers gave detailed accounts a few days earlier, represented an imminent and extremely grave danger. In consequence, his elimination was decided upon and organized with savage cunning.

And the ferocious crime, which made a tremendous impression everywhere, would have remained wrapped in the deepest mystery, primarily in compliance to the deplorable yet insufficiently deplored principle of *omertà*, if the seizure of the copy of the cable sent from Partinico by Carlo Costantino to Giuseppe Morello of New York—

"I Lo Baido work Fontana"—had not thrown a flash of glaring light into the shadowy areas of our inquiries.

That curt cable of only four words was a revelation and acquired exceptional importance when the sender and the recipient were identified; and when, with respect to them, all the grave facts were coordinated with those detailed in reports previously submitted by me.

Carlo Costantino and Antonino Passananti returned unexpectedly from America, passing off their sudden journey with the excuse that they sought thereby to escape payment of some petty debts. Actually, both brought large sums of money to Italy and only a short time before Costantino had announced that he had established himself permanently in Brooklyn, where he had had a house of his own built and furnished with luxurious furniture and decorations.

Costantino, who by his own admission traveled under a false name, stated that he had landed at Le Havre, whereas we have found that he landed at Naples. Questioned about the mysterious cable, he preferred not to explain why he had not signed it and why he had refused to give his own address to the telegraph office. Of the mysterious message, he tried to create the impression that he and a certain Lo Baido were supposed to buy wine on behalf of Fontana, but then he had no explanation for having sent the cable to Morello (whom he professed not even to know by sight) instead of to Fontana. Furthermore, in spite of all our efforts, we have found no trace of any Lo Baido who has anything to do with wine and is known by Costantino.

Certain photographs found on Costantino are interesting. In one of them there is a view of a shop in New York under the firm name of Pecoraro-Lo Baido. In fact, I have a suspicion that the Lo Baido of the New York firm of Pecoraro-Lo Baido and the Lo Baido of the cable are in reality Antonino Passananti, who, perhaps, as is the custom in America, was hiding under this name.* Proof of this, however, I have not found, and, for the moment, therefore, I cannot rule out the possibility that this may be someone else. None the less it is worth noting that Passananti disappeared on the morning of March 12, the day on which Petrosino was killed in Palermo. I must further mention in this connection the anonymous letter sent from Brooklyn, which

---

*It is unfortunate that Commissioner Ceola did not know that, after the "barrel murder," Costantino used the name of Pecoraro. In that case his suspicion would have become certainty.—Author.

has already been brought to your knowledge, and in which it is clearly stated that the "Partinicans" Costantino and Passananti were assigned to carry out the crime.

As far as Vito Cascio Ferro is concerned, I beg to inform you that my men are looking for him.

To sum up: we have the proof that Cascio Ferro was afraid that Petrosino was looking for him; this is confirmed by his disappearance from Bisaquino and the memorandum written in pencil by the American lieutenant in which Cascio Ferro is referred to as a dreaded criminal. We also have the result of the searches undertaken in Costantino's domicile, the statements and explanations by him that have been proved false; the disappearance of Passananti on the day of the murder; an anonymous letter addressed to the American consul, Bishop, that names Morello as the instigator of the crime; the three anonymous letters sent to me in which Cascio Ferro, Costantino, and Passananti are accused.

All these pieces of evidence, already quite important in themselves because based on matters of fact, complement one another perfectly when put together and assume the quality of direct proof, manifest and unquestionable.

As for the motive for the crime, I believe that after what I have set forth it may be stated that complete light has been shed.

We come now to the actual perpetrators of the homicide. Two were certainly the direct killers; the collaborators and accomplices were many, required not only for the completion of the act but also to expedite the escape of the killers. All these persons I think I have included among the seventy whom I ordered arrested. There are thirteen old criminals, except of course for Cascio Ferro, Costantino, and Passananti, the list of whom I enclose and whom I beg to accuse before this most honorable Indictment Division as responsible for the murder of Lieutenant Giuseppe Petrosino.

The Commissioner
Baldassare Ceola*

---

*The report of the Police Commissioner of Palermo, with its wealth of felicitous insights and documented evidence, persuaded the officials of the Indictment Division to order the thirteen suspects transferred from preliminary custody to arrest for trial, while two warrants of arrest were issued for Cascio Ferro and Passananti.—Author.

14. *"For Lack of Evidence"*

DON VITO CASCIO FERRO was arrested in Bisaquino in the after-noon of April 3. He had just gotten off a train and was hurrying back to his house by carriage when he saw Di Stefano, the deputy agent-in-charge, and his supervisor, Salvatore Ponzio, coming to-ward him with a special policeman, Benedetto Chillé.

"I didn't know anyone was looking for me," he said when the warrant for his arrest was shown to him, "or I should have ap-peared on my own volition." Don Vito, who had had three weeks in which to prepare himself for this meeting and to weigh his line of defense, seemed quite sure of himself. "I'm sure there's been some misunderstanding," he added, with a conciliatory smile. "In any event, please consider me completely at your disposal."

"We've been looking for you for some time, Don Vito," Ponzio said. "Your absence had frightened us. Where have you been?"

"In Burgio, of course. That's where I've been living for several months, and just the other day I filed papers to establish residence in that town."

"But isn't it here that you have a house?" Ponzio asked.

"Indeed yes, sir," Don Vito replied in his usual polished tone. "My wife lives here—poor woman, she's been paralyzed for years—and my old father is here; and, as you certainly would not have neglected to find out, I also have a mistress and an illegitimate son in Bisaquino. But you will agree with me that none of this prevents me from choosing to be officially domiciled where I prefer."

"But do you have a house in Burgio?" the agent in charge persisted. Ponzio was unable to guess where Don Vito was leading in his line of defense.

"No, not yet," Cascio Ferro said quietly. "But I intend to register my domicile as the Honorable De Michele Ferrantelli's house. As you know, I've been working for him for some time. I have made some contribution, however modest, to his recent election, and in return he honors me with his esteemed protection."

Di Stefano, alarmed by the turn that the conversation was taking, tried to break in. "These things," he said, "would be better discussed in Palermo, in front of the Commissioner."

"At your service," Don Vito assented, with a slight bow, but he immediately added in a voice suddenly turned dominating: "In any case, let it be quite clear that I, from March 6 to 14, was constantly, day and night, inside the house of the Honorable De Michele. He himself will corroborate this if it is necessary."

"An ironclad alibi," Ponzio remarked in a tone as sarcastic as it was discouraged.

While Vito Cascio Ferro was being taken to Palermo, Di Stefano was making a thorough search of his house. At its conclusion he formally took custody of the following items:

—One photograph taken in New York, showing Carlo Costantino, Mr. and Mrs. Giuseppe Morello, Vito Cascio Ferro, Antonino Tamburello, Giuseppe Zito, Mario Maniscalco, Domenico Pasqua Ragusa (an engineer), Giacomo Ganci, Francesco Aiello, Giu-

seppe Fontana, Aurelio Bonomi, and Mr. and Mrs. Paolo Valzer
—One picture postcard sent from New York, with this message:
"Affectionate kisses and a prosperous future from your friend
Riccobono"
—One photograph of two women, with an inscription in English
sign "Tillie"
—One letter from Brooklyn, reading as follows: "Dear Don Vito,
I send you news of my perfect health, as I hope to hear of yours.
I'd like to know how our business came out: I want it all de-
scribed. I greet you most heartily. Vincenzo Di Leonardo"
—One letter from Ribera, dated March 29, 1909, with this cryptic
message: "My very dear friend signor Don Vito. You will do me
the service of sending to have your dog picked up.* I am always
distracted and the dog wants to play because he is young while
I would like to find somebody who could help me get through
this time, which I have a bellyful of. Your always affectionate
friend Emanuele Geraci"
—One visiting card belonging to "Vito Lo Baido son of Domenico,
Brooklyn"
—One steamship ticket from New Orleans to Palermo, dated September 28, 1904
—One note of four lines written in English, signed *Sophie Bresci*.
[This was the widow of the man who killed Umberto I.] Un-
fortunately the note has since been lost, and it had not occurred
to anyone to translate it into Italian. It is also strange that
Baldassare Ceola, even though he had had dealings with Gaetano
Bresci in Monza, should have neglected to look into the mysteri-
ous connection between Don Vito and the assassin's widow.

Later Cascio Ferro was subjected to personal search in Palermo,
and an official copied two documents found in his pockets. But
these turned out merely to be notes taken by the many-sided Don
Vito to prepare defenses for men under his protection who had got

---

*The investigators suspected that the "dog" in question was actually the
fugitive Antonino Passananti, but it was not possible to prove this.—Author.

into trouble over cattle stealing. Here, none the less, are the curious memoranda:

Giuseppe Voltaggio

Good record. Tells things honestly. Sergeant [of Carabinieri] believes he is telling the truth. First puts up refusal. Why? No prior agreement. Agreement in past. Counterfeiting of brand. Tusitante (?) Article 366. Confirms good faith. Had no animals. Lo Bianco gives no orders to remove the animals. His Excellency Toto is nearby.

Antonio Lombardo

Two charges: forgery and receiving stolen property (twice). No forgery. Receipt for 158 lire. Female donkey from legitimate source. Receiving stolen sheep. Why it was seized from him. Robbery. Restitution of donkey and receipt. Receiving. Good faith. Bought at fair. Verbal quarrel. Fair at Dolo. Animal count: 115 sheep, 24 lambs: one third allowance turban (?). Price 12.50 lire. Goats 32, allowance one third, amounts to 8.50 lire. 1500 lire—1500 and more, 1610 lire. Removal to country. Letter received and telegram they arrested. No surveillance! ! ! Forte. Pizzo. Lo Bello. Russo. Up to 15–16. From one to four years. Good record (carrying weapons).

During his interrogation in Police Headquarters Don Vito Cascio Ferro once again displayed complete self-assurance. He repeated that he had stayed with the Honorable De Michele Ferrantelli from March 6 to 14. He added that on the fifteenth he had gone to Sciacca, still with the Honorable De Michele, to look into the award of a certain railway construction contract and that finally he had gone back to Bisaquino, unaware that the police were looking for him.

It should not be necessary to add that, when the Honorable De Michele Ferrantelli was questioned in his turn, he confirmed on his honor the story told by Don Vito.

Don Vito was then shown the various photographs and papers found in his house, but he refused to sign the official report of their seizure. "You could have found them somewhere else," he said. Asked for explanations of the photograph in which he was shown with Giuseppe Morello, Don Vito said he did not know anyone named Morello. "I don't remember when the picture was taken," he added. "Obviously this gentleman who you say is Giuseppe Morello was merely one of the many casual acquaintances I had when I lived in New York."

At the end of the interrogation he refused also to sign the innocuous transcript of the testimony. "I have no intention of signing any document," he announced firmly, "just as I have no intention of making any further statements. If I have anything more to say, I'll say it in court."

That same evening Don Vito was placed in a cell that already contained his fourteen supposed confederates. He asked for a paid cell* and was also given permission to have his meals sent in from a nearby restaurant.

While Vito Cascio Ferro seemed very sure of himself, Baldassare Ceola, on the other hand, did not seem so confident. The Police Commissioner of Palermo was naturally convinced of the validity of his charges; none the less, knowing Sicily and, above all, knowing the character of the man whom he had ordered arrested, he had sound reasons for fearing some unpredictable setback that would shatter the whole structure of the case that he had so patiently built up.

Therefore, even after the inception of the formal pretrial investigation, Ceola continued with his own, seeking both to track down Antonino Passananti and to gather further evidence of the guilt of the fifteen men in his cells. But it was not possible for him to carry his work to its conclusion. The setback that he feared came at the psychological moment, even though not in a wholly unpleasant fashion.

On July 17, three months after Petrosino's murder, Baldassare Ceola received a dispatch from Rome informing him bluntly that he had been relieved of his duties and was being recalled to the capital. A few days later he was formally placed in retirement with the honorary title of Prefect of the Realm, as his nephew, Professor Federico Curato of Milan, recalled. Ceola died on April 1, 1913.

---

*Available, under the prevailing regulations, to those who had the money to purchase privacy.—Translator.

By a singular coincidence, July 17, 1909, was a decisive day too for Police Commissioner Theodore Bingham of New York. For some time his opponents in the Board of Aldermen—in other words, almost the entire membership, which had fought the creation of his secret police—had been joined in a coalition against him. And now, after Petrosino's death, Bingham had finally lost his few allies as well. Alone, he was exposed to the attacks of enemies who accused him of careerism, of a lust for publicity and, above all, of having doomed at its start, through his disclosures to the *Herald,* the already risky mission assigned to Petrosino. He came before the Board on the evening of July 17 as a defendant rather than as a high official.

He tried to defend himself by shifting a great part of the responsibility to the ineptitude of the Italian police and to the efficacy of the "Black Hand." He added that the story of Petrosino's journey had been seized on by a reporter for the *Herald* who had wormed his way into Bingham's confidence and abused it. In conclusion he declared that, in any case, the Black Hand certainly had other sources of information without having to rely on the *Herald.*

Bingham's plea in his own defense had no effect whatever on his judges and their reaction was extremely harsh. Speaking for all of them, Alderman Doull said: "From what I can find out, the real killer of Petrosino is you, Commissioner Bingham. The story of his trip to Italy came from your office at 300 Mulberry Street, and it is in that office that we must look for the man responsible for the brave lieutenant's death."

Exercising the powers of his office, the Mayor of New York removed Theodore Bingham that same night from his post as Police Commissioner. This was the end of his political career.

After Ceola's departure, the preliminary investigation of the case against Don Vito and his supposed accomplices took a turn that at once showed clearly that everything was going to be settled with a dismissal of the charges. Within a few months all the suspects were set free—some on probation, some on bail. At the same time, it was necessary to postpone the liquidation of the investigation until the sensational case had been deflated and public opinion had been diverted to other matters. And it is understandable that to the Americans, accustomed to seeing suspects brought before the courts within a few days of their arrests,* these procedural delays should have seemed more than questionable. The final decision—which called for quashing the charges against all the suspects—was handed down more than two years later, on July 22, 1911. It did not evoke the slightest reaction in the press, which at that time was too deeply involved in the approaching war against Libya that broke out two months afterward.

It is, unfortunately, impossible to reconstruct the progress of the interminable pretrial investigation. The entire record of the matter, in fact, has vanished from the archives of Palermo, and with it have disappeared also the transcripts of interrogations, voluntary statements, documents, other evidentiary material, and the formal complaint by the Public Prosecutor.

On the other hand, I have managed to find a handwritten copy of the order quashing the charges as it was handed down by the magistrates of the Indictment Section of the Palermo Courts. Its text is puzzling. All the accused were set free for lack of evidence, the classic formula whenever charges against Mafiosi were involved. And yet, even from that very order, it is clear that the evidence against at least the three principal suspects was quite substantial. Hence one cannot understand how, in a case of such importance, the examining magistrates could have refused to send it to trial and allowed the Court of Assizes to decide whether the evidence was sufficient.

In the name of His Majesty
VITTORIO EMANUELE III
by the grace of God and the will of the Nation King of Italy
The Court of Appeals of Palermo, Indictment Division, composed of Signori Nicola Nicofora, presiding, and Giuseppe La Mantia and Nicola Ratti, counselors, on this day of July 22, 1911, convened in

---

*Some sixty years ago this was indeed true of American criminal justice.—Translator.

chambers to consider the charges laid by the Public Prosecutor with regard to the case against:

Paolo Palazzotto, Ernesto Militano, Salvatore Seminara, Camillo Pericò, Francesco Pericò, Pasquale Enea, Giovanni Ruisi, Carlo Costantino, Giuseppe Bonfardeci, Giuseppe Fatta, Giovanni Dazzò, Giovanni Finazzo, Gaspare Tedeschi, Vito Cascio Ferro, and Antonino Passananti, accused of voluntary homicide with aggravating circumstances, by means of firearms, committed in Palermo on the night of March 12, 1909, against the person of Giuseppe Petrosino, lieutenant of the police of New York.

Having heard the report of Cavalier Cannada, Deputy Public Prosecutor, who, prior to his withdrawal, left before us the records of the case and the written accusations of the Public Prosecutor, Cavalier Mercadante, _____ [sic] finds that early in March of 1909 Giuseppe Petrosino, lieutenant of police of the City of New York, debarked in Palermo. He was charged with a mission and had first of all to obtain here in Sicily a file of information and penal records concerning various Sicilian emigrants who, on the other side of the ocean, in the great North American Republic, appear to be, are directly shown to be, or are suspected of being the authors of those numerous crimes that, because of a characteristic peculiar to all of them, are grouped together under the label of "Black Hand": that is, robbery, abduction, threatening letters, bomb-throwing, etc.

In order better to carry out his mission and avoid investigation by those whose interest it was to wreck his project, Petrosino was traveling under a false name, which, however, he was not able to preserve in dealing either with the American consul or with the various Italian authorities with whom he was obliged to confer, not to mention the fact that among the great number of emigrants who have come back from America it was not impossible or even very unlikely that some of them, encountering Petrosino, would recognize him.

And indeed it was fact that he was recognized by various persons on his visits to the office of the American consul in Palermo. Nor was this his only indiscretion, which is almost inexplicable on the part of a detective as well known as Petrosino.

Although the Police Commissioner of Palermo put plainclothesmen at his disposition, he refused this courteous and prudent suggestion. Nor is this all: even though he knew that Piazza Marina was a meeting place for repatriated emigrants, he insisted on taking up residence in the Hôtel de France and on having his meals regularly in the Oreto restaurant, each of which is situation in the aforesaid Piazza Marina.

On the evening of March 12, having returned from Caltanissetta, he went to dine at the Oreto, after which he went out into the square, where he was accosted and wounded by more than one shot.

Long and painstaking investigations were carried out with a view to finding the authors of the crime. Unfortunately, the Mafia and the *omertà* that torment and poison the minds of the Sicilian masses (who see in the murder of a policeman merely the execution of a legitimate punishment), the remarkable negligence that the police of New York showed in conducting the investigations with which they had been charged by the Italian authorities, the inadequacy of the American judicial system, which (when it chose to do so) was capable of replying in superlatively unresponsive fashion to our pressing and numerous requests for information, all this contributed to preserving the thickest veil round the authors of the crime.

Meanwhile, as the arrests of the first suspects were being carried out, the investigation was extended to the passengers who had traveled with Petrosino on the same vessel and to others who had arrived from America immediately prior and immediately afterward, but the results of these inquiries were negative.

At the conclusion of the prolonged and arduous pretrial investigation, only a few indications of criminal responsibility emerged relative to the accused Palazzotto, Militano, Seminara, Pericò Camillo and Francesco, Enea, Ruisi, Bonfardeci, Fatta, Dazzò, Finazzo and Tedeschi. Wherefore, as to these accused, it must be found that there is no possibility of proceeding further for lack of sufficient evidence.

Against Carlo Costantino, however, there are indications of guilt, but they do not appear to be sufficient to persuade the Indictment Division to remand him for trial, and the same may be said of Antonino Passananti and Vito Cascio Ferro. These evidences of guilt, in relation to Costantino, consist of his capacity for crime, his flight from New York under a false identity, his arrival in Sicily almost simultaneously with Petrosino's, his sudden wealth, his enigmatic cablegrams through which he shows himself to be a friend of two notorious Sicilian criminals residing in the United States (Giuseppe Morello and Giuseppe Fontana), the first of whom is now serving a long sentence for extortion and counterfeiting of currency.

All the evidence that is applicable to Costantino is equally applicable to Passananti, who returned from America with Costantino and who was always with him during their stay in Sicily. In addition, his name, like Costantino's, appears in the notebook found in Lieutenant Petrosino's pocket and he is listed there as a fierce criminal.

With regard to Vito Cascio Ferro, whom Costantino stated that he did not know, it must be noted that suspicions arose against him immediately. He is one of the most notorious Mafiosi and it has been shown that in the United States he, with the abovementioned Costantino, Morello, Fontana, and others designated as chiefs of the Black Hand, formed a dangerous band on which watch was kept with special attention by Petrosino himself. It is likewise shown that more than once Costantino went to confer with Cascio Ferro both in Corleone and in Bisaquino, while the purpose and the content of these conversations have not been plausibly explained by them.

In any case, as has already been stated, the said evidence is not sufficient to order the three accused remanded for trial. Therefore Costantino, Passananti, and Cascio Ferro shall be relieved of the restrictions imposed on them at the time of their imprisonment, and the restitution to them of the sums paid in as bail is hereby ordered.

Though this decision officially wrote finis to the investigation into the murder of Lieutenant Petrosino, the matter remained open for many years to come. From every part of the world accusations, disclosures and confessions having to do with the mysterious crime continued to pour in. These communications, although very often containing matters useful to general police records on various dangerous criminals, turned out to be of no value toward the solution of the case. However, they bear witness to the tremendous interest aroused in all countries by the murder of the famous policeman. Furthermore, Petrosino was by now a figure of legend; this is shown by the hundreds of books, pamphlets and comic-strip magazines that gained worldwide circulation and that made the Italian-born detective the hero of the most miraculous adventures. Hollywood itself even devoted a film to him, *Pay or Die,* in which he was portrayed by Ernest Borgnine.

Of all these disclosures, only one, in all honesty, should have been given greater consideration—that by the former chief of the "Black Hand" of New York, Giuseppe Morello, made when he was a federal prisoner in Atlanta in 1911. But here a brief preamble is necessary.

After the death of Petrosino and the ouster of Bingham, the new Police Commissioner of New York, William F. Baker, issued instructions to one of his deputies, Flynn (the same man who had worked with Petrosino on the "barrel murder"), to reopen the investigation into Morello and Ignazio Lupo on the old charge of counterfeiting, which had been dropped. According to Baker, this was the only vulnerable point at which the two gangsters could be attacked.

The new investigation was indeed successful. Incredibly, witnesses who had suffered from total amnesia at the trial six years earlier now suddenly got their memories back. All the efforts of the defense lawyers were of no use. Giuseppe Morello was sentenced to twenty-five years in prison and Ignazio Lupo was sentenced to thirty. Both were sent to the Federal Penitentiary in Atlanta.

In actuality it was the very Mafia of which they were members that caused Morello and Lupo to be convicted. The witnesses had regained their memories simply because no one had told them to keep their mouths shut. Morello himself charged that he was the victim of a betrayal. And indeed his "throne" had already been under serious threats from aspirants younger and better equipped than he. These pretenders were Jim Diamond Colosimo, Giuseppe Masseria (called "Joe the Boss"), and Johnny Torrio, godfather of a little boy named Alfonso Capone and known as Al.

Giuseppe Morello's "revelations," therefore, were probably dictated by a desire for revenge. The fact remains, however, that in March 1911 he asked to talk to Deputy Commissioner Flynn and tell him everything about Petrosino's murder. He said that Passananti and Costantino, who had fled to Italy to avoid arrest, immediately supposed that Petrosino had come to Sicily in search of them, and therefore they had turned to Vito Cascio Ferro and requested his protection. Morello added that it was Don Vito who had planned the trap. He had begun by infiltrating his own men into Petrosino's confidence, and finally he himself had played the part of stoolpigeon, promising the detective his full collaboration.

According to Morello, in sum, on the night of March 12 Petrosino had an appointment in Piazza Marina with Cascio Ferro himself, and it was Don Vito himself who killed him.

Giuseppe Morello made this statement to Flynn under a pledge of confidentiality, but he told him also that he was prepared to sign such a statement. By the next day, having got the information no one knows from whom, the Italian newspapers in New York printed the story. Then, probably, Morello received threats of reprisal in prison; or he had other reasons for backing down on his decision. The fact remains that, when Flynn returned with a public official, the gangster refused to sign any statement at all.

Other "revelations" were received by the thousands. Police Headquarters in Palermo alone got about three thousand. The most recent arrived in 1967.

This voluminous collection has accumulated into a thick file that is still kept in the archives in Palermo. The material contained in it has often proved useful in the solution of other cases or in reconstruction of the biographies of notorious criminals.

15. Don Vito's "Confession"

MANY YEARS LATER at a time when he no longer had anything to lose since—for reasons that will appear—he was in prison, Vito Cascio Ferro said that it was he who had killed Joseph Petrosino. "In my entire life," he declared, "I have killed only one person, and that I did *disinterestedly*." This would seem to imply a matter solely of prestige: Petrosino had defied the Mafia by going to Sicily to investigate, and it was incumbent on the head of the honorable society to respond. "Petrosino," Don Vito said also, "was a courageous enemy; he did not deserve a dirty death at the hands of just any hired killer." And this would mean that he himself killed the detective.

Though in my opinion there is no doubt that Cascio Ferro was the organizer of the crime, and probably the actual executioner as well, it must be recognized that these statements, as well as others that he made toward the end of his life, are susceptible to challenge. First, to be accurate, Don Vito never made a regular, proper confession; he always confined himself to "giving to understand," in the typical Mafia language that tells and does not tell, that alludes to concrete facts but in a context that is vague and difficult of verification. Second, not only did he have nothing to lose but, given his mentality, he had everything to gain. The execution of the Number One Enemy of the Black Hand of New York indubitably added luster to his escutcheon as former head of the Mafia of Sicily. And, finally, it is difficult to distinguish between the statements that he actually made and those that have been attributed to him, inasmuch as neither kind were ever officially recorded. This, in fact, was the period just before World War II. Fascist Italy boasted of having extirpated the Mafia and, at the same time, she was flirting with its sons who had made a place for themselves in America with their machine guns; it was forbidden for criminals in American films to have Italian names and, at the same time, Benito Mussolini appointed Vito Genovese, the head of Cosa Nostra in the United States, to be a Commendatore del Regno—Knight of the Realm. It was therefore on political grounds that it was deemed proper not to reopen the case. No one wanted to give the foreign press an excuse to revive an anti-Italian campaign.

None the less, the news of Don Vito's "confession" reached America, even though greatly delayed. On July 6, 1942—in the midst of the war—*The New York Times* and *The Sun* announced to their readers that the "Petrosino case" had finally been solved. Under the significant headline WHEN MUSSOLINI WAS USE-FUL, *The Sun* summarized the entire affair and paid tribute to Prefect Mori, who, having brought about the arrest of Vito Cascio Ferro and his subsequent trial and conviction (though for a different crime), had "avenged the great detective's death." Therefore, because of the course of the war, nothing further was printed. Petrosino had been forgotten for some time and the world had quite different matters on its mind.

As I have said, the precise tenor of Cascio Ferro's statement is very debatable. The most widely known version dealing with the execution of the crime, which is generally accepted by historians of the Mafia, is the one according to which Cascio Ferro went off in a carriage to kill Petrosino. For example, one writer said that on that day Don Vito "was a guest of a deputy from Palermo who was giving a reception to celebrate his victory at the polls. At a certain time Don Vito left the house by carriage, reached Piazza Marina, where Petrosino was waiting for him, and killed him after a brief exchange. The murder done, the killer returned to the home of his host, who, not having noticed his absence, subsequently corroborated his alibi in all good faith." This version, which I believe to be accurate in the essentials, nevertheless contains an error. Don Vito was indeed the guest of the Honorable De Michele Ferrantelli, but in Burgio and not in Palermo, and Burgio is at least forty-five miles from Piazza Marina. Therefore his was an absence not of a few minutes but of several hours. In consequence it is permissible to harbor some doubt as to the good faith of the deputy who corroborated his alibi.

But what happened to the fifteen men whom Ceola, having completed his investigation into the murder of Petrosino, had accused of having acted in concert to commit homicide? This question can be answered as a result of a documented study by a journalist, Nicola Volpes, published by *Il giornale di Sicilia* on the anniversary of the detective's death.

Let us leave for the end the story of the "decline and fall" of Don Vito and let as start with Antonino Passananti, the only one of the fifteen who escaped arrest in 1909. On April of 1911, a few months after the end of the pretrial investigation, the police staged a hunt in the area of Sciacca where it was supposed that he was hiding with his brother, Giuseppe, and with Nicolò Lo Manto, the brother of his fiancée, Rosalia. Passananti was not found, but he turned up shortly afterward at San Cipiriello, where he killed one Calogero Vaccaro in revenge and seriously wounded the victim's brothers, Natale and Salvatore. For this crime he was sentenced *in absentia* on June 19, 1912, to thirty years. A few months later there was another piece of theater. As a result of undisclosed secret arrangements, Passananti let it be known that he was prepared to give himself up. And so he did, demanding that the agent in charge of public safety in Partinico, Augusto Battioni, go to fetch him with a carriage. Apparently Passananti knew what he was doing when he made up his mind to turn himself in to the police. Four years later, in August 1916, he was turned loose again in spite of the long prison sentence. Thereafter there was no sign of him for many years. In 1926 he was accused of criminal association, forgery and corruption of a public official, and he was officially reported to be a fugitive and in hiding. In 1933 he turned up again to demand the return of a Fiat sports car that had been seized from him. In 1934 his driver's license was revoked because of his convictions for homicide, passport falsification, harboring of criminals, etc. Another long period of silence ensued until 1961 when, at the age of eighty-three, Passananti came out of oblivion again to request and obtain the restoration of his driver's license. This much-desired paper was again revoked, in 1968, this time for reasons of health. A few months later, on March 6, 1969, a short piece in the newspapers reported that "Antonino Passananti, old-age pensioner, killed himself in his home in Partinico by shooting himself in the temple." And another newspaper man observed: "It is sad to think that he took his life just when he was about to be accepted into society again." Passananti had initiated rehabilitation proceedings, and a police report from Partinico stated that "he no longer associates with criminal figures. He can no longer be regarded as a socially dangerous individual." He was ninety years old.

Gaspare Tedeschi, Don Vito's friend, had assorted ups and downs. Known to the police as an anarchist and then as the head of the Mafia in Villafrati, Mezzojuso and Baucina, he managed to get himself elected mayor of Villafrati. He was granted a full pardon in 1926 by Mussolini, to whom he at once sent a telegram: "Released from prison this very day. In the joy of finding myself embraced by my children, to you, Duce, I dedicate my first thought. Ready to immolate ourselves for you and for your ideas with loyalty and ineradicable devotion." Altogether, Tedeschi had been named in twelve warrants of arrest for robbery, three homicides, arson, extortion, counterfeiting, etc. In 1950, shortly before his death, he was convicted of diverting gas and electric current. The downhill road.

Giovanni Ruisi, who had returned from the United States in 1908—deported at the hands of Petrosino—left Sicily again after the murder. He was arrested in Marseilles, Algeria and Tunis. In 1920 he was back in New York, an influential figure in local criminal life. Returning to Italy for good, in 1935 he opened a butcher shop in Palermo. His method of operation was highly profitable—interfered with by no one, he simply carried off whatever meat he needed for his business and did not bother to pay for it. The loss was distributed equally among the other butchers, who simply paid twenty centesimi more per kilogram.

Giovanni Battista Finazzo, born in 1879, had been accused of murder in 1908 by Joseph Petrosino. The victim was Epifanio Arcara, an immigrant found dead of thirty-two stab wounds and mutilation of his genitals. When the detective arrived in Palermo the case was still open. It was dismissed in 1910 by the New York courts, in the defendant's absence, for lack of evidence. Known to the Carabinieri as a "criminal without scruples in the service of the Mafia," Finazzo managed, between crimes, to insinuate himself into the good graces of Alessandro Cardinal Lualdi, who appointed him to membership in the building committee for the shrine of Santa Rosalia on Mount Pellegrino.

Paolo Palazzotto has not left much about himself in the police files. A victim of alcoholism, he was always involved in brawls. He died in 1958. Nor did Pasquale Enea, who died in 1951, leave much of a file. He had a record for running an illegal lottery, damage to property, bankruptcy, swindling, forgery and physical violence.

Giovanni Dazzò was also a former resident of Little Italy. Convicted of attempted homicide, he had an unsettled score with Petrosino who on a number of occasions had intervened to protect Mrs. Dazzò, the former Fanny Favarino, from her husband's savage beatings. They had had other encounters too, and in the end Petrosino had managed to have Dazzò thrown out of the country.

Salvatore Seminara, Camillo and Francesco Pericò, Giuseppe Fatta and Giuseppe Bonfardeci are figures of no great interest. They had all been convicted for the same joint crime—counterfeiting American currency—and they were old associates of Giuseppe Morello. One thing is interesting: in a police report Bonfardeci is described as Palazzotto's "favorite" friend.

Carlo Costantino was born in Partinico on January 20, 1874. He married Rosalia Casarubbia and they had three children. Then he lived with a woman called Carmela, with whom he had more children. The Carabinieri wrote of him: "Innate tendency to crime, idleness, debauchery, vagrancy." He had a record of criminal association, attempted homicide, robbery, forgery, swindling, etc. Arrested on March 19 in the Petrosino case, he was released on the following November 13. Subsequently he moved to Ravenna, and then to Bardonecchia where he was arrested in a series of swindles. Sentenced to the Ucciardone Prison in Palermo, he told the prison doctor, Di Liberto, that he had contracted syphilis at the age of thirty and suffered ever since from buzzing in the ears and lapses of memory as a result of the treatments he had undergone. In 1932 he was deported to Lampedusa,* where he spent four years, setting up an illegal liquor business. On his return to Palermo he opened a feed warehouse in Via del Fervore. He died soon afterward in a mental hospital, riddled with syphilis.

After the dismissal of the charges of having killed Petrosino, Vito Cascio Ferro resumed his former operations undisturbed. He had a brilliant career and became the greatest *capo* that the Mafia had ever had. His name is still famous in Sicily even today. For some fifteen years he *governed* the western part of the island without encountering the slightest hindrance, bringing the organization to its highest pinnacle. He even succeeded in setting up a fleet of trawlers to be able to transport stolen cattle to African markets without interference.

Don Vito ruled mainly by making use of his natural power over people; he resorted to violence, with ruthless coldness, only when

---

*One of the islands in the Mediterranean to which the Fascists sent both political and criminal prisoners.—Translator.

it was necessary. As he grew older he assumed an almost royal
manner, and he was, in actuality, a kind of king. The rich feared
him, the peasant masses idolized him; and, of course, he had the
talent for winning confidence and respect through gifts, charities,
redress of minor wrongs. For this reason Don Vito came to enjoy
not only the absolute obedience of his Mafiosi but also the uncon-
ditional backing of the authorities. Under him the peasants lived
well, no one took the risk of striking, and, if any rash union agitator
tried to "stir up the workers," Don Vito's long arm got to him
ahead of the Carabinieri.

In those years of great success Vito Cascio Ferro did not think
in terms of self-enrichment, completely caught up as he was in the
exciting exercise of power. He had a son by a mistress (*paramour*
was the word he used under questioning, according to the transcript) whom he had originally hired to help his paralyzed wife.
He was very fond of this boy and sent him away to school, keeping
him isolated from his own world with that typical aspiration among
Mafia *capi* to turn their sons into gentlemen.

His kingdom began to totter about 1923. In that year the sub-
prefect of Corleone wrote to the Minister of the Interior: "He is one
of the worst old criminals. He is completely capable of committing
any crime. Honest people live in holy terror of him. Strengthened
by the fact that he is at the head of a powerful criminal association
ready to defend him by any and all means, he has devoted himself
to crime with utter dedication. I am citing him for application of
the *ammonizione*. Unfortunately, as a result of that unhappy plague
omertà, no one, not even the most courageous and the most honest,
will come forward to testify against him. A powerful criminal organization is active behind him and is ready to defend him, and
therefore no one will dare to take the risk of catching a volley of
bullets for the pleasure of giving conscientious testimony. . ."

The communication from the subprefect of Corleone had no
sequel. In 1924 the Police Commissioner of Palermo not only rejected the move for the *ammonizione* but, refusing as well even to
revoke Cascio Ferro's gun permit, described him as a "model citizen,
honest, hardworking, and respectful toward the authorities."

But it was the beginning of the end. After 1924, with the consolidation of the Fascist dictatorship, the Mafia found itself cut off. It lost both the support of the political class, which had abdicated in favor of the dictatorship, and that of the landowning class, which, now that the government was guaranteeing "social stability," no longer needed *men of respect* to keep the peasants in line.

In May 1925 Vito Cascio Ferro was arrested, with forty-year-old Vito Campegna of Prizzi, for the murders of Francesco Falconieri and Gioacchino Lo Voi, both of whom were guilty of having rebelled against the extortions of the Mafia. Don Vito was accused of having ordered the murders and Campegna of having carried them out.

In other days Don Vito would have gotten out of trouble on this charge too, with a dismissal for lack of evidence. And indeed he had no problem obtaining his release on bail. But barely a year later Prefect Mori arrived in Sicily to launch his operations against the Mafia. The island was laid waste by fire and sword, many of the innocent suffered with the guilty, and no great distinction was made between enemies of law and order and enemies of Fascism. Thus Don Vito was arrested again and, after four years of pretrial detention, tried in the Court of Assizes in Agrigento on a charge of *moral complicity* in the double murder. On July 6, 1930, he was convicted and sentenced to nine years in solitary confinement.

Since the Fascists had instituted extremely harsh restrictions on the publication of crime news, the Italian press did not even mention the matter. None the less, Prefect Mori took it on himself to make it public. He wanted everyone to know the end to which the powerful Don Vito had come and, in the style of the old Far West, he had posters printed with the criminal's photograph and the text of the sentence; these were then put up on walls everywhere on the island. Only one American newspaper printed the story of the sentence of "the murderer of Petrosino."

According to a popular legend, Don Vito continued to exert great influence even from prison, but this is probably not true, From the Ucciardone, where he was truly revered by the other inmates (it was said that on the wall of his cell he had written with a nail: "Prison, illness, and poverty show us the heart of a real friend"), he was very soon transferred to Portolongone and then to the penitentiary in Pozzuoli, where he remained for the rest of his life.

Thus, like his life, Don Vito's death was surrounded by an aura of mystery. I succeeded in establishing that he died in the summer of 1943 at the age of eighty-one; but two years later, in 1945, he was still officially recorded as being alive. Actually, that was the year in which his petition for royal clemency, submitted many years earlier, reached the desk of the Police Commissioner of Palermo. The Commissioner rejected the petition on the ground that, "The act of clemency might provoke acts of reprisal on the part of relatives of the persons whom he caused to be killed."

The explanation for this strange episode is to be found in the confused state of affairs prevailing in the summer of 1943. Fascism had collapsed, the Allied armies were moving north along the peninsula, and the Flying Fortresses were attacking without respite; so the prison authorities had ordered the evacuation of the penitentiary of Pozzuoli, which was too exposed to bombardment. In a few hours all the inmates were moved except one; Don Vito, who was *forgotten* in his cell.

He died of thirst and terror in the gloomy, abandoned penitentiary, like the villain in some old serial story.